Home Cooking

WITH **AMY COLEMAN**

Volume 4

Based on the Public Television Series
SPONSORED BY KITCHENAID

Home Cooking

WITH AMY COLEMAN

Volume 4

Produced by Marjorie Poore Productions

Photography by Alec Fatalevich

Contents

Introduction

This book contains the recipes prepared on the fourth season of the "Home Cooking" series, a national public television cooking program, which features a guest cookbook author every week. We draw from a pool of some of the most talented and interesting cookbook authors in the country. Year after year, we marvel at the abundance of new ideas and wonderful recipes that keep coming from these authors. They demonstrate just how dynamic and fascinating the world of cooking is, whether you are pursuing it as a hobby or as a professional. This year we had an especially exciting group.

We were honored and delighted to have the grande dame of Italian cooking, **Marcella Hazan**, and her book, Marcella Cucina. Marcella was the first to show Americans back in the '70s what real Italian food was all about and ignited a love affair that continues to thrive well past the infatuation stage. Besides Marcella, we were blessed with another Italian maestro, **Lynne Rossetto Kasper**, who has garnered award after award for her coverage of Italian regional cooking. Her latest is The Italian Country Table, the result of years of travel and research into the homes of some of the best Italian home cooks. Our last stop in Italy took us south with Naples at Table, courtesy of renowned food writer **Arthur Schwartz**, who has produced a remarkable work on the food of Campania, the cradle of Italian-American cuisine.

When it comes to cuisine, we don't play favorites and thus turned our sights on France. Our escort was the food editor of Saveur magazine, **Colman Andrews,** who, through the magazine's latest book, Saveur Cooks French, reaffirmed the belief that French food is the number one cuisine in the world. Guest **Michael Roberts** also stands firm on this ranking having spent years studying Parisians' passion for food and putting the results into a terrific book called Parisian Home Cooking. Our last stop in that part of the world was with one of San Francisco's star chefs, **Gerald Hirigoyen**, who grew up in Basque country, a region which straddles France and Spain and whose cuisine represents an exciting mix of both cultures.

On the other end of the cuisine spectrum, two equally gifted authors, **Eileen Yin-Fei Lo** and **Nina Simonds**, aptly represented Asian cooking. Eileen's book, The Chinese Kitchen, demonstrates fundamental principals of Chinese cooking, with such important basics as the right way to cook rice. Nina, on the other hand, focused on the Asian belief that food has healing powers, curing everything from high blood pressure to anxiety. We also found that her recipes in A Spoonful of Ginger can cure just about any hungry appetite.

Besides our international experts, we had a number of home-grown authors who didn't need a passport to find great cooking. From the Napa Valley, acclaimed cooking teacher, **Hugh Carpenter**, made some Fast Appetizers — also the name of his latest book —and a sampling from his comprehensive and "finger-licking good" Great Ribs Book. California chefs **Sara Corpening** and **Mary Corpening Barber**, returned as guests to share with us some tasty selections from their Cocktail Food and Wraps books; pure California and pure delicious. Another Golden State representative — or should we say senator — **James McNair**, made us a fabulous meal from James McNair's Favorites, pulling together the best of his over 30 cookbooks.

Regional American cooking was well represented this year as well. **Joyce White** compiled a priceless collection of recipes from African-American churches across the nation in her

Soul Food *cookbook. From El Paso, Texas, we had a visit from* **Park Kerr** *who showed us why they call it "supper", not "dinner" down there with a style that is relaxed and food that is spicy and delicious. Speaking of spicy guests,* **Biker Billy** *and his latest book,* Freeway-A-Fire, *showed us that he spends as much time in the kitchen as he does on his Harley. Not a single recipe from Biker Billy lacked a chile — not even his peach cobbler dessert. From up North, we got some up-scale Philadelphia food from Chef* **Jim Coleman**, *author of* The Rittenhouse Cookbook *who makes healthy, low-fat food taste like the real thing. But for the real thing, we went to a place in Brooklyn, New York, where no one gives a care about calories or cholesterol. The place is Junior's, one of the most famous diners in America.* **Alan Rosen** *shared secret recipes handed down to him from his grandfather for Junior's cheese-cake, beef brisket, and potato pancakes. Another taste of New York came from* **Susan Friedland**, *who put together a wonderful collection of celebratory meals in her book called* Shabbat Shalom. *You don't have to be Jewish to appreciate and use the wonderful recipes in this book.*

Bruce Aidells *opened all our eyes with his latest work,* The Complete Meat Cookbook, *just the guide and cookbook everyone needs to take them into the new millenium of meats which are 30 percent leaner than 10 years ago. Your old recipes may just not work anymore. Another new generation cookbook we are thrilled to include in the series is* Electric Bread for Kids, *a work from a remarkable woman,* **Ann Parrish**, *who understands how kids can have real fun in the kitchen. Another believer of kids in the kitchen is* **Paul Newman** *who, with his buddy, A. E. Hotchner, produced* Hole in the Wall Gang Cookbook, *a great collection of recipes from their world-famous camps.*

We love to grill on Home Cooking and had two exciting guests who brought a whole new dimension to outdoor cook-ing. **Steven Raichlen**, *who has traveled extensively all over the world collecting grilling recipes, cooked from his newest opus,* The Barbecue! Bible. **Jamie Purviance**, *another grill master who can keep anyone glued to his or her grill, filled the studio air with the irresistible smells of grilling with recipes from* Weber's Art of the Grill *cookbook, a beautiful cookbook that every grilling aficionado should have.*

For dessert, we had a couple of showstoppers. **Nick Malgieri**, *shared some of his favorites from his* Chocolate *book, includ-ing the world's best brownies.* **Rose Levy Beranbaum**, *the patron saint of pastry and author of the* Cake Bible *and* The Pie & Pastry Bible, *made some divine offerings which would keep anybody's god happy.* **Bruce Weinstein** *with his Ulti-mate Ice Cream Book showed us how to recapture the kind of wonderful, rich homemade ice creams found in ice cream par-lors of the past. He also showed us how to make some of those trendy sorbets that have captured everyone's attention recently.*

Marlene Sorosky, *a frequent guest on and source of endless ideas, once again demonstrated why she's our guiding light when it comes to holiday entertaining. She showed us an assortment of holiday gifts that can be made right in the kitchen. She also made a wonderful Christmas dinner with some unusual twists.*

Finally, our mini-chef, **Jennifer**, *who has graduated to "midi" status as she approaches her teens, picked another great kids' book,* Classic Cookies, *from the ever-prolific Klutz Press.*

I hope these recipes bring you as much excitement and inspi-ration as they did for us. I can assure you every one of them is delicious.

——Marjorie Poore, Producer

STARTERS

Mushrooms Stuffed with
Goat Cheese, Spinach and Bacon

MARY CORPENING BARBER AND SARA CORPENING WHITEFORD / REPRINTED FROM *COCKTAIL FOOD* (CHRONICLE)

4 tablespoons plus 2 teaspoons bacon
   grease or olive oil
1 cup chopped onion
3/4 teaspoon kosher salt
1/2 teaspoon freshly ground black pepper
8 ounces goat cheese, at room temperature
2 tablespoons heavy cream

1/4 teaspoon ground nutmeg
One 10-ounce package frozen chopped
   spinach, thawed
1/2 pound bacon, cooked and finely
   chopped
36 white mushrooms, uniform in size,
   stems removed

✳ Preheat the oven to 350°F.

✳ Heat 2 teaspoons of the bacon grease or olive oil in a medium nonstick skillet over medium heat. Add the onion and season with 1/4 teaspoon of the kosher salt and 1/8 teaspoon of the pepper. Sauté until the onion is tender, 5 to 7 minutes. Transfer to a medium bowl and let cool. When cool, add the goat cheese, cream, nutmeg and 1/8 teaspoon of the pepper. Stir until well mixed.

✳ Squeeze the spinach with your hands to remove any excess liquid. Add the spinach and bacon to the onion mixture. Refrigerate until ready to use.

✳ Heat 2 more tablespoons of the bacon grease or olive oil in a large nonstick skillet over medium heat. Add 1/2 of the mushrooms and season with 1/4 teaspoon of the kosher salt and 1/8 teaspoon of the pepper. Sauté the mushrooms until golden brown and tender, about 4 minutes per side. Transfer to a paper towel-lined baking sheet, top side up. Wipe the skillet with a paper towel and return to the heat. Add the remaining mushrooms and season with the remaining 1/4 teaspoon kosher salt and the remaining 1/8 teaspoon pepper. Transfer to the baking sheet with the other mushrooms.

✳ To assemble, place 1 heaping teaspoon of the spinach filling in the center of the bottom of each mushroom. Bake until warm, 5 to 7 minutes. Serve warm.

DO AHEAD TIPS: The spinach filling can be prepared up to 2 days in advance and refrigerated. The mushrooms can also be assembled up to 2 days in advance and refrigerated. Bake as directed.

MAKES 36 STUFFED
MUSHROOMS

THIS IS A FOOLPROOF RECIPE FOR pleasing A CROWD. SELECT MUSHROOMS THAT ARE SLIGHTLY LARGER THAN bite-size. THEY WILL SHRINK A LITTLE WHEN THEY ARE cooked, BUT ANYTHING BIGGER CAN BECOME MESSY.

Toasted Pecan and English Stilton Napoleons

MARY CORPENING BARBER AND SARA CORPENING WHITEFORD / REPRINTED FROM *COCKTAIL FOOD* **(CHRONICLE)**

MAKES 48 NAPOLEONS

THESE BITE-SIZED SAND-

WICHES ARE ambrosia

FOR CHEESE AND NUT

LOVERS. AND THE PRESEN-

TATION IS impressive

FOR SUCH A SIMPLE-TO-

PREPARE HORS D'OEUVRE.

IF YOU REDUCE THE

RECIPE, DO NOT USE A

FOOD PROCESSOR; MAKE

THE CHEESE mixture

BY HAND. CHOP EXTRA

CHIVES AND SPRINKLE

THEM ONTO A PLATE AS

A colorful BACKDROP

FOR THE NAPOLEONS.

96 perfect pecan halves (about 5 ounces)
3 ounces cream cheese, at room
    temperature
2 ounces Stilton cheese, at room
    temperature

2 teaspoons port wine
1/2 teaspoon honey
Pinch of freshly cracked black pepper
2 tablespoons chopped fresh chives,
    for garnish

✳ Preheat the oven to 350°F.

✳ Place the pecans on a baking sheet. Bake until brown and aromatic, 7 to 10 minutes. Remove the pecans from the oven and let cool.

✳ Combine the cream cheese, Stilton, port, honey, and pepper in a food processor. Process until smooth. Transfer to a locking plastic bag and squeeze the mixture into one corner of the bag.

✳ To assemble, spread 48 pecan halves flat-side down on the baking sheet. Cut a small tip off the corner of the bag of cheese mixture. Pipe about ¼ teaspoon of the cheese mixture evenly onto each pecan half. Top with a second pecan half, flat side down, and pipe about ¼ teaspoon of the cheese mixture onto each napoleon. Sprinkle with chopped chives to garnish.

DO AHEAD TIPS: The pecans can be toasted up to 3 days in advance and stored in an airtight container. The Stilton mixture can be prepared up to 3 days in advance and refrigerated; bring it to room temperature before assembly. Assemble the napoleons up to 3 hours in advance and let stand at room temperature.

Middle Eastern Eggplant Puree with Tahini

STEVEN RAICHLEN / REPRINTED FROM *THE BARBECUE BIBLE* **(WORKMAN)**

MAKES ABOUT

2¹/₂ CUPS; SERVES 8

CHARRING THE EGGPLANT ON THE grill IMPARTS AN INTENSE SMOKE FLAVOR TO THE EGGPLANT. SERVE THIS VERSION OF baba ghanoush AS A dip WITH PITA CHIPS.

2 long, slender eggplants (about 2 pounds total)

9 cloves garlic, 8 cut lengthwise in half and 1 minced

2 green onions, white and green parts, trimmed and finely chopped

3 tablespoons tahini (sesame paste)

3 tablespoons extra-virgin olive oil, or more to taste, plus 1 tablespoon for serving

3 tablespoons fresh lemon juice, or more to taste

Salt and freshly ground black pepper to taste

Grilled Pita Chips (*recipe follows*)

❋ Preheat the grill to high. Using the tip of a paring knife, make 8 small slits in each eggplant and insert a half-clove garlic in each slit. Set the eggplants aside.

❋ When ready to cook, place the eggplants on the hot grate and grill, turning with tongs, until the skin is charred all over and the flesh is very soft, 20 to 30 minutes; the eggplants will have lost their firm shape. Transfer the eggplants to a plate to cool.

❋ With a paring knife, scrape the charred skin off the eggplants. Transfer the eggplant flesh to a food processor. Add the minced garlic, green onions, tahini, 3 tablespoons oil, 3 tablespoons lemon juice, and salt and pepper and process until smooth. Taste for seasoning, adding salt, oil, or lemon juice as necessary; the mixture should be very tangy.

❋ Spoon the dip into a serving bowl and drizzle with the remaining 1 tablespoon oil. Scoop up the dip with the pita chips.

Grilled Pita Chips

3 large or 4 small pita breads

3 tablespoons extra-virgin olive oil

1 tablespoon regular or black sesame seeds (optional)

❋ Preheat the grill to high. Cut larger pitas into 8 wedges, smaller pitas into 6 wedges (see note). Generously brush both sides of each wedge with oil. Sprinkle one side of each wedge with sesame seeds, if using.

❋ When ready to cook, arrange the pita wedges on the hot grate and grill, turning with tongs, until nicely browned, 1 to 2 minutes per side. Place the wedges in a single layer on a tray, platter or cake rack and let cool. The wedges will crisp on cooling. *Makes 24 wedges.*

NOTE: For extra-crisp chips, separate each pita into two rounds by cutting it in half horizontally. Cut each round into wedges, brush on both sides with oil (you'll need more oil) and grill. This gives you a thinner, and therefore crisper, pita chip.

Catalan Tomato Bread

STEVEN RAICHLEN/REPRINTED FROM *THE BARBECUE BIBLE* **(WORKMAN)**

4 fresh, very ripe tomatoes, cut in half
4 cloves garlic, cut in half (optional)
8 slices country-style bread,
    cut 1/2-inch thick

Cruet of extra-virgin olive oil
Small bowl of course salt (kosher or sea)
Freshly ground black pepper (optional)

* Preheat the grill to medium-high.

* Place a half tomato and half garlic clove, if using, on each serving plate. When ready to cook, arrange the bread slices on the hot grate and grill until nicely browned, 2 to 4 minutes per side.

* Place a piece of grilled bread on each plate. To eat, rub a bread slice with the cut garlic, if using, then with the cut tomato. Drizzle each slice with oil and sprinkle with salt and pepper, if desired. Serve immediately.

SERVES 8

THERE ARE TWO ways TO SERVE TOMATO BREAD. THE first IS FOR THE COOK TO DO THE RUBBING AND drizzling. THE second IS TO PROVIDE EACH PERSON WITH A clove OF GARLIC, HALF TOMATO, cruet OF OIL AND BOWL OF SALT AND LET HIM OR HER DO THE WORK. THE second WAY IS MORE fun.

Cured Salmon, Cream Cheese and Caper Wraps

MARY CORPENING BARBER AND SARA CORPENING WHITEFORD / REPRINTED FROM *WRAPS* (CHRONICLE)

1/2 cup cream cheese, softened
2 tablespoons capers, drained and slightly chopped
1 tablespoon prepared horseradish
1/8 teaspoon freshly ground black pepper
Two 10- or 11-inch flour tortillas

1 cup (about 6 ounces) gravlax or smoked salmon, cut into thin strips
2/3 cup peeled and chopped cucumber
1/2 cup chopped fresh fennel fronds
1/4 cup chopped fresh dill
2 tablespoons chopped red onion
2 teaspoons extra-virgin olive oil

✱ Combine the cream cheese, capers, horseradish and 1/8 teaspoon pepper in a small bowl and mix well. Divide the filling among the tortillas and spread evenly over each tortilla, leaving at least a 1-inch border around the edge.

✱ Mix together the remaining ingredients in a medium bowl.

✱ Divide the salmon mixture among the tortillas and fold in the sides of each tortilla. Fold up the bottom of each tortilla and continue to roll up into a cylinder, enclosing the filling. Cut the wraps in half on the diagonal and serve.

California Wrap

MARY CORPENING BARBER AND SARA CORPENING WHITEFORD / REPRINTED FROM *WRAPS* (CHRONICLE)

1 teaspoon powdered wasabi
1 teaspoon water
1 tablespoon soy sauce
2 cups cooked short-grain rice, at room temperature, or substitute medium-grain rice
1/4 cup seasoned rice vinegar
3/4 pound fresh crabmeat, picked over

1 cup chopped avocado
1 cup peeled and chopped cucumber, seeds discarded
1/2 cup sliced green onion, green part only
1/4 cup chopped pickled ginger
2 tablespoons mayonnaise
Four 10- or 11-inch flour tortillas
4 sheets nori

✱ Dissolve the wasabi in the water in a small bowl. Add the soy sauce. Combine this mixture with the rice in a large bowl. Add the vinegar and gently stir in the crabmeat, avocado, cucumber, green onion, ginger, and mayonnaise.

✱ Line each tortilla with a sheet of nori. Divide the rice mixture among the nori-lined tortillas and fold in the sides of each tortilla. Fold up the bottom of each tortilla and continue to roll up into a cylinder, enclosing the filling. Cut the wraps in half on the diagonal and serve.

Tic-Tac-Toe Quesadillas

REPRINTED FROM *THE HOLE IN THE WALL GANG COOKBOOK* (SIMON AND SCHUSTER)

One 12 1/2-ounce can tuna fish, drained
9 to 10 black olives, (6 chopped, and 3 to
  4, without pits, sliced into 12 circles,
  3 to 4 circles per olive)
1 medium-sized green onion, sliced
1/2 cup sour cream, at room temperature
8 flour tortillas

1 cup whole-kernel yellow corn
1 pound cheddar cheese, grated
3/4 cup Newman's Own Medium Salsa, or
  your favorite
1 1/3 cups grated Monterey Jack cheese
2 small cans mild green chiles, cut into
  thin strips

✻ Preheat the oven to 350°F. Coat 2 large baking sheets with nonstick cooking spray.

✻ In a small bowl, combine the tuna fish, chopped olives, green onion and sour cream and mix well. Set aside.

✻ Place 2 tortillas on each of 2 baking sheets. Divide the tuna mixture evenly among the 4 tortillas, putting a dab in the center of each and spreading evenly out to the edges.

✻ Layer each tortilla with 1/4 cup of the corn, 1/4 of the grated cheddar cheese and 3 tablespoons of the salsa.

✻ Place the remaining 4 tortillas on top of the 4 on the baking sheets and sprinkle with Monterey Jack cheese. Arrange the chile strips in a tic-tac-toe grid on each, and fill each grid with 3 olive circles.

✻ Bake for approximately 15 minutes, until the cheese melts and the quesadillas are heated through. Cut into wedges to serve.

Quesadillas with Barbecued Meat and Brie

HUGH CARPENTER/REPRINTED FROM *FAST APPETIZERS* (TEN SPEED)

¹/₄ pound Chinese barbecued pork	Two 10-inch flour tortillas
¹/₂ papaya, not quite ripe	¹/₄ cup purchased barbecue sauce
¹/₄ pound Brie cheese	¹/₄ cup chopped fresh cilantro
1 whole green onion, minced	¹/₂ tablespoon unsalted butter

✱ Cut the meat into very thin slices. Peel, seed and very thinly slice the papaya. Cut the Brie into very thin pieces. The preparation can be completed to this point 8 hours prior to cooking.

✱ Place a tortilla on the counter. Rub the surface with ½ of the barbecue sauce. In even layers, add ½ each of the meat, papaya, Brie, green onions and cilantro. Cover with another tortilla and press firmly. Set aside on a plate.

✱ Place a 12-inch skillet over medium-high heat. When hot, add the butter. When the butter melts and becomes light golden, add the quesadilla to the pan. Cook until golden, about 30 seconds. The quesadilla will have a better texture if you place a small plate on top of the quesadilla during cooking. Turn the quesadilla over and cook for another 30 seconds with a weight on top.

✱ You can refrigerate the quesadillas at this point. Reheat in a 500°F. oven for 5 minutes.

✱ Cut the quesadillas into wedges. Transfer to a serving platter and serve immediately.

SERVES 6 TO 10

TO save TIME, USE YOUR OWN BARBECUE SAUCE, AND PURCHASE THE BARBECUED (OR ROASTED) meat FROM A NEARBY MARKET. THESE APPETIZERS ARE ALSO good MADE WITH SUPERMARKET ROAST CHICKEN OR THINLY SLICED roast BEEF. YOU CAN ALSO COOK THESE ON THE BARBECUE, OR BAKE THEM IN A 400°F. oven UNTIL HEATED THROUGH.

Marinated Goat Cheese with Garlic, Basil and Orange Zest

HUGH CARPENTER/REPRINTED FROM *FAST APPETIZERS* (TEN SPEED)

SERVES 6 TO 10

IT'S THE infused OIL THAT GIVES THE GOAT CHEESE AN INTENSE AND exciting FLAVOR. YOU CAN VARY THE TYPE OF peppercorns USED, OR SUBSTITUTE MINT OR CILANTRO FOR THE BASIL. THIS marinated GOAT cheese IS ALSO VERY GOOD SERVED IN BELGIAN ENDIVE CUPS.

One 12-ounce log soft goat cheese, chilled
3/4 cup extra-virgin olive oil
1 tablespoon whole tricolor peppercorns
1 teaspoon whole allspice berries
2 cloves garlic, finely minced
2 tablespoons finely minced fresh ginger
1/3 cup slivered fresh basil leaves
1 teaspoon grated orange zest
30 crackers, your favorite type

✴ Using a thin-bladed vegetable knife or paring knife, cut the goat cheese into ½-inch-thick slices. Place each slice in a single layer in a Pyrex pie plate or baking dish. Dip the knife blade in very hot tap water after each cut.

✴ In a small saucepan, combine the oil, peppercorns and allspice. In a small bowl, combine the garlic, ginger, basil and orange zest. Place the saucepan over medium-high heat and cook until the peppercorns begin to "pop," about 2 minutes. Immediately stir in the garlic mixture. After 5 seconds of stirring, pour the hot oil mixture over the cheese. Marinate the cheese in the refrigerator for at least 3 hours. This can be done up to 1 week prior to serving.

✴ When the cheese is still chilled, transfer the cheese to a decorative plate. Pour the oil over the top. Serve chilled or at room temperature with crackers.

Baked Tomatoes Stuffed with Salmon, Garlic and Capers

MARCELLA HAZAN / REPRINTED FROM *MARCELLA CUCINA* (HARPERCOLLINS)

1 tablespoon capers, preferably packed in salt

1 pound salmon

3 1/2 tablespoons extra-virgin olive oil

1 tablespoon chopped fresh Italian parsley

1 teaspoon very finely chopped garlic

2 tablespoons fine, dry, unflavored bread crumbs

Salt and freshly ground black pepper to taste

2 large, ripe, firm tomatoes, weighing approximately 3/4 pound each

✹ Drain the capers if packed in vinegar; soak, rinse and drain if packed in salt. Chop the capers finely.

✹ Preheat the oven to 400°F.

✹ Remove the salmon's skin, remove any loose membranes, and carefully pick out all bones. Cut the fish into very small dice and put it in a bowl together with 2½ teaspoons of the olive oil, the parsley, garlic, capers, 1 tablespoon of the bread crumbs, salt and several grindings of black pepper. Toss thoroughly.

✹ Wash the tomatoes, cut them in half horizontally and scoop out all the seeds and the centers to make a cup-like hollow. (If you are cooking anything else that day or the next that calls for fresh tomatoes, use the scoopings in the recipe.)

✹ Pat the inside of the tomatoes with paper towels to soak up excess juice, then stuff them with the salmon mixture, pressing it down lightly as you do so. There should be enough to form a mound. Sprinkle the tops with the remaining bread crumbs and drizzle with the remaining olive oil, holding back a few drops to smear on the bottom of a baking pan.

✹ Place the tomatoes in the baking pan and bake in the upper level of the preheated oven for 35 minutes, or until the salmon stuffing has formed a light golden crust. Serve not piping hot, but lukewarm. They are also good later, at room temperature, but not reheated.

SERVES 4

THIS MAKES AN ELEGANT AND **unexpected** APPETIZER, THOUGH IT'S **simple** TO PREPARE AND WON'T KEEP YOU CONFINED TO THE KITCHEN AT **party time**.

Salmon Gefilte Fish

SUSAN FRIEDLAND/REPRINTED FROM *SHABBAT SHALOM* **(LITTLE, BROWN)**

One 6- to 7-pound salmon, skinned and filleted, head and bones reserved, or 3 to 4 pounds salmon fillets and heads and bones from 2 salmon
6 onions, quartered
2 tablespoons kosher salt
2 teaspoons freshly ground white pepper
5 carrots, peeled and coarsely chopped
4 large eggs, lightly beaten
1/4 cup matzo meal
Lettuce leaves
Red or white horseradish

✳ Slip a paring knife between the flesh and the skin of the salmon and gently separate the two, using a sawing motion. Put the skin, bones, and head of the salmon in a large pot (an 8- or 9-inch Dutch oven is perfect) with 3 of the quartered onions, 1 tablespoon of the salt, 1 teaspoon of the white pepper and the carrots. Cover with 4 quarts of water and bring to a boil over high heat. Reduce the heat to low, partially cover the pot and simmer for at least 1 hour or up to 2 or 3 hours. Occasionally skim the foam the rises to the surface of the liquid.

✳ Cut the salmon into cubes, checking each piece for any bones that may remain. Grind the salmon cubes in a food processor, using the metal blade and pulsing to get the right texture—tiny pieces, not a puree. Transfer the fish to a large mixing bowl.

✳ Add the remaining 3 quartered onions to the work bowl of the processor. Finely chop the onions and add them to the fish along with the eggs, matzo meal, and the remaining salt and pepper. Stir just to combine.

✳ With moistened hands, make oval dumplings using 1/4 cup of the fish mixture for each. Place the dumplings on a platter and refrigerate for at least 30 minutes or up to 2 hours.

✳ With a long-handled skimmer, gently drop the fish balls into the simmering liquid. Don't crowd the pan—if necessary, cook the fish in batches, keeping the waiting ones in the refrigerator. Cover the pot and poach the fish dumplings at a quiet simmer for about 30 minutes, until they are firm and cooked. They will rise to the top of the liquid as they cook. With a slotted spoon, transfer the fish to a deep platter or wide bowl. When all of the fish is cooked, bring the stock to boiling. Reduce it to about 2 cups. Pass the stock through a very fine sieve and strain it over the fish. Let the fish cool and refrigerate it until cold, at least 4 hours, preferably overnight, to give the liquid enough time to gel.

✳ To serve, place 2 fish dumplings on a lettuce leaf for each serving. Serve with red or white horseradish.

Salmon Cakes

JOYCE WHITE / REPRINTED FROM *SOUL FOOD* (HARPERCOLLINS)

1 pound cooked salmon, fresh or canned
1 small onion
1 beaten egg
1/2 cup soft bread crumbs
1 tablespoon Worcestershire sauce
1/4 to 1/2 teaspoon hot pepper sauce
1/4 teaspoon freshly ground black pepper

1 cup shredded sharp cheddar cheese
1 tablespoon finely chopped fresh Italian
  parsley
1/4 cup flour
4 tablespoons (1/2 stick) butter or
  margarine
Lemon wedges

✳ If using canned salmon, drain and pick over carefully to remove any dark cartilage and bones. Fincly chop the onion.

✳ Using a fork, flake the salmon (removing any bones you may find) and then combine it in a medium bowl with the onion, egg, bread crumbs, Worcestershire sauce, hot sauce, black pepper, cheese and parsley.

✳ Using about 1/3 cup salmon mixture for each cake, shape the mixture into rounds about 1/2-inch thick.

✳ Sprinkle the flour on a plate or board. Dredge the cakes in the flour, coating well, but dusting off excess flour.

✳ Place the cakes in the refrigerator and let set for 30 minutes or longer.

✳ Heat the butter or margarine in a large skillet until foamy and hot. Add the cakes and brown on both sides, cooking about 5 minutes.

✳ Remove the salmon cakes from the pan and drain on paper towels. Serve warm immediately, with lemon wedges.

SERVES 4

THE NEXT TIME YOU PREPARE salmon STEAKS FOR DINNER, MAKE A FEW EXTRA AND SAVE THEM TO MAKE THESE delicious SALMON cakes, OR CROQUETTES. THEY'RE EASY TO PUT together AND CAN EVEN BE PREPARED ahead OF TIME, BUT BE SURE TO SERVE THEM HOT, JUST AFTER COOKING.

SERVES 4

IN ANY DISCUSSION OF
BASQUE CUISINE, THIS DISH
IS ALWAYS MENTIONED
AS A signature DISH
OF THE REGION. THERE,
TYPICAL PEPPERS WOULD BE
THE ROASTED piquillo
peppers OF LODOSA,
WHICH CAN BE FOUND
CANNED IN specialty
MARKETS IN THIS COUNTRY.

Peppers Stuffed with Salt Cod

GERALD HIRIGOYEN / REPRINTED FROM *THE BASQUE KITCHEN* (HARPERCOLLINS)

1 pound salt cod
3/4 cup olive oil
1 large onion, finely diced
4 cloves garlic, minced
1 dried New Mexican chile, seeded and cut
 into 1/2-inch pieces
Kosher salt to taste

Freshly ground white pepper to taste
4 roasted red bell peppers, peeled
 and cored
1 cup flour
2 eggs, lightly beaten
2 cups fine dried bread crumbs
1 tablespoon chopped fresh Italian parsley

✱ Soak the salt cod in cold water to cover for 24 to 48 hours, changing the water 3 to 4 times, to desalt according to taste. Drain and pat the salt cod dry. Cut it into 5 to 6 large pieces, removing the bones, and set aside.

✱ Heat 1/2 cup of the olive oil in a large skillet over medium-high heat. Add the onion, garlic and chile and sauté until the vegetables are translucent, about 5 minutes. Add the cod, reduce the heat slightly and cook for 5 minutes, swirling the pan occasionally.

✱ Increase the heat slightly and cook the mixture for 5 more minutes, continuing to swirl the pan every few minutes to mix the ingredients. Pour the contents of the pan into a colander suspended over a bowl to drain. Reserve the cooking liquid (*jus*) and set aside. Remove and discard the chile. Season the mixture with salt and pepper.

✱ Gently smash together the onion and cod, using the back of a large spoon. Remove any remaining bones as you work. Gently fill the peppers with the cod stuffing until full, taking care not to break the peppers; set aside.

✱ Preheat the oven to 400°F. Over medium-high heat, warm the remaining 1/4 cup of the olive oil in an ovenproof skillet.

✱ Place the flour, beaten eggs and bread crumbs into separate shallow dishes. Dredge the stuffed peppers in the flour, dip them into the eggs, then roll them in the bread crumbs. Place the peppers in the skillet and brown them on one side for 2 to 3 minutes. Turn them over and place the pan in the oven until the peppers are hot throughout and golden brown all over, 5 to 7 minutes.

✱ Warm the cod *jus* in a small saucepan over high heat. Add the parsley and swirl the pan until the jus boils.

✱ Place one pepper in the center of each of 4 serving plates. Spoon the cod *jus* evenly around the peppers. Garnish with a few turns of the pepper mill.

Chipotle-Rock Shrimp Salad in Tortilla Cups

MARY CORPENING BARBER AND SARA CORPENING WHITEFORD / REPRINTED FROM *COCKTAIL FOOD* (CHRONICLE)

2 tablespoons vegetable oil
3/4 pound (about 1 1/2 cups) rock shrimp
1/2 teaspoon kosher salt
1/8 teaspoon freshly ground black pepper
1/2 cup cream cheese, at room temperature
2 tablespoons chopped fresh cilantro
1 tablespoon plus 2 teaspoons lime juice
1/2 teaspoon minced garlic

1 teaspoon minced canned chipotle chiles in adobo sauce (*see note*)
1/2 teaspoon dried oregano
1/4 teaspoon onion salt
1/2 cup fresh uncooked corn kernels
1/3 cup diced red bell pepper
Three 8-inch flour tortillas
48 cilantro leaves for garnish

✻ Heat 1 tablespoon of the oil in a large skillet over high heat. Season the shrimp with 1/4 teaspoon of the kosher salt and the pepper. Sauté the shrimp over high heat, stirring occasionally, until the shrimp turn pink, 2 to 3 minutes. Transfer to a strainer and let cool. When cool, chop the shrimp coarsely.

✻ Combine the cream cheese, cilantro, lime juice, garlic, chipotle chiles, oregano and onion salt in a medium bowl. Stir until well mixed. Add the corn, red pepper and shrimp and mix well. Refrigerate until slightly chilled.

✻ Preheat the oven to 350°F.

✻ Place the tortillas in a stack and trim the edges to form a 6-inch square. Brush both sides of each tortilla with the remaining 1 tablespoon oil. Restack the tortillas and cut each into 16 squares.

✻ Press each square firmly into the bottom of miniature muffin tins (1-inch cups). Season with the remaining 1/4 teaspoon kosher salt. Bake until golden brown, about 10 minutes. Let cool.

✻ To assemble, fill each tortilla cup with 1 teaspoon of the shrimp mixture. Garnish with a cilantro leaf and serve.

DO AHEAD TIPS: The shrimp salad can be prepared 1 day in advance. The tortilla cups can be prepared up to 5 days in advance and stored in an airtight container. Assemble as directed.

NOTE: Canned chipotle chiles in adobo sauce can be found in supermarkets and Latino specialty markets.

MAKES 48
FILLED TORTILLA CUPS

ROCK SHRIMP IS WONDERFUL FOR stuffings AND COLD SALADS THAT ARE BOUND WITH CREAM CHEESE OR MAYONNAISE. IT IS FULL OF flavor AND MUCH MORE ECONOMICAL THAN LARGER SHRIMP OR PRAWNS. ALSO, YOU DON'T HAVE TO PEEL AND DEVEIN ROCK SHRIMP, WHICH IS A REAL time SAVER.

Wok-Seared Beef in Endive Cups

HUGH CARPENTER/REPRINTED FROM *FAST APPETIZERS* (TEN SPEED)

1/2 pound beef tenderloin
1 tablespoon hoisin sauce
1 tablespoon oyster sauce
1 tablespoon dark sesame oil
1 tablespoon Chinese rice wine or
   dry sherry

1 teaspoon Asian chili sauce
3 cloves garlic, finely minced
2 whole green onions
1/4 cup fresh mint leaves
20 large endive cups
2 tablespoons flavorless cooking oil

✳ Trim and discard all the fat from the meat. Cut the meat across the grain in the thinnest possible slices. Overlap the slices and cut into 1/4-inch-wide matchstick-shaped pieces. Transfer the meat to a bowl and add the hoisin sauce, oyster sauce, sesame oil, rice wine, chili sauce and garlic. Mix thoroughly and refrigerate. Shred the green onions and mint leaves; combine and refrigerate. Set aside endive cups. The preparation can be completed to this point up to 8 hours in advance of the last-minute cooking.

✳ Place a wok over the highest heat. When the wok becomes very hot, add the cooking oil. Roll the oil around the sides of the wok. As soon as the oil begins to smoke, add the beef, separating the pieces and cooking until all the beef just loses its raw outside color. Add the green onions and mint. Stir-fry for another 15 seconds.

✳ Slide the mixture onto a platter. Ring the platter with endive cups. Serve at once. Each person spoons a little of the filling into an endive cup, and eats the cup using their fingers.

SERVES 6 TO 12

STIR-FRYS MAKE great APPETIZERS. THE PREPARA-TION CAN BE COMPLETED HOURS IN ADVANCE, AND THE LAST-MINUTE COOK-ING TAKES ONLY SECONDS. ANY stir-fry RECIPES CAN BE CONVERTED INTO AN APPETIZER. JUST DICE OR MATCHSTICK-CUT ALL THE MAIN INGREDIENTS SO THEY WILL easily FIT INTO AN ENDIVE LEAF OR other TYPE OF LETTUCE CUP.

SIDE DISHES

Peanutty Coleslaw

JAMES MCNAIR/REPRINTED FROM *JAMES MCNAIR'S FAVORITES* (CHRONICLE)

1 head cabbage (about 1 1/2 pounds)
1 cup homemade or high-quality
    purchased mayonnaise
1/2 cup Asian sesame oil
1/3 cup smooth peanut butter, at room
    temperature
3 tablespoons unseasoned rice vinegar or
    white wine vinegar

2 tablespoons freshly squeezed lemon
    juice
1 tablespoon soy sauce
Salt and freshly ground black pepper
    to taste
Hot chile oil to taste
1 tablespoon unsalted butter
1 cup unsalted dry-roasted peanuts

✳ Discard any wilted outer leaves from the cabbage. Rinse the cabbage under cold running water. With a food processor or a sharp knife, shred the cabbage thinly and place it in a large bowl.

✳ In a food processor or blender, combine the mayonnaise, sesame oil, peanut butter, vinegar, lemon juice and soy sauce and blend well. Season to taste with salt, pepper and chile oil. Pour the mixture over the cabbage and toss thoroughly. Cover and let stand at room temperature for about 2 hours, or refrigerated for up to 24 hours; bring the slaw to room temperature before serving.

✳ In a skillet, melt the butter over low heat. Add the peanuts and cook, stirring frequently, until the peanuts are golden brown and fragrant, about 3 minutes; watch carefully to prevent burning. Transfer to paper towels to drain and cool.

✳ Just before serving, stir in most of the peanuts, saving a few to sprinkle over the top.

SERVES 8

Outstanding WITH
BARBECUED OR GRILLED
MEATS, ESPECIALLY BABY
BACK RIBS, THIS slaw
TASTES best WHEN
PREPARED A FEW HOURS BE-
FORE SERVING. BE SURE TO
bring IT BACK TO ROOM
TEMPERATURE
BEFORE SERVING.

ANY VARIETY OF GREEN
cabbage CAN BE USED
ALONE, OR COMBINED
WITH DIFFERENT TYPES OF
CABBAGE FOR diversity
IN COLOR AND FLAVOR.

SERVES 6

HERE'S A beautiful

PUREE THAT'S easy

TO PREPARE AND REALLY

dramatic ON

THE PLATE.

Beet Puree

SUSAN FRIEDLAND / REPRINTED FROM *SHABBAT SHALOM* (LITTLE, BROWN)

1 1/2 to 2 pounds beets
10 to 14 whole, unpeeled garlic cloves
3 tablespoons olive oil
2 tablespoons wine vinegar

1 tablespoon sugar
Salt and freshly ground black pepper
   to taste

✳ Preheat the oven to 450°F. Trim the green beet tops to 1 inch and scrub the beets well. Wrap the beets with aluminum foil and roast for about 1 hour and 15 minutes, until tender. When cool enough to handle, slip off the beet peels with a paring knife (wear plastic gloves to prevent staining your hands with the juices) and cut into quarters.

✳ Wrap the garlic cloves in aluminum foil and roast them along with the beets.

✳ Put the cooked beets in a food processor. Squeeze the garlic cloves out of their skins into the processor. Add the olive oil and process until smooth. Mix in the wine vinegar, sugar, salt and pepper. Taste for seasoning. If making ahead, cool the puree, cover and refrigerate until ready to serve.

✳ Reheat the beet puree gently and serve.

SERVES 4 TO 6

SEPHARDIC IN

inspiration, THIS

DISH IS GOOD WITH

roast CHICKEN AND

FISH, AND EVEN AS A

first COURSE.

Sautéed Spinach with Currants and Pine Nuts

SUSAN FRIEDLAND / REPRINTED FROM *SHABBAT SHALOM* (LITTLE, BROWN)

2 pounds spinach
3 tablespoons pine nuts
2 tablespoons olive oil

1 tablespoon minced garlic
3 tablespoons dried currants
Salt and freshly ground black pepper
   to taste

✳ Wash and stem the spinach. You needn't dry it, but drain it well.

✳ Toast the pine nuts in a cast-iron skillet over medium heat. Watch carefully—they go quickly from pale to burned.

✳ Heat the oil in a large skillet. Add the garlic and sauté for 2 to 3 minutes. Stir in the currants and then the spinach. Cover the skillet and cook for 5 minutes, until the spinach is wilted. Season with salt and pepper; toss in the pine nuts and serve.

Sautéed Garlic Greens

JOYCE WHITE / REPRINTED FROM *SOUL FOOD* (HARPERCOLLINS)

3 pounds collard greens
1/4 to 1/3 cup vegetable oil
1 large onion, chopped
2 to 3 cloves garlic, minced

1/2 to 1 cup chicken broth
3/4 teaspoon salt
1/2 teaspoon freshly ground black pepper

✹ Pick over the greens and discard any with yellowing or wilted leaves. Remove any thick stems. Stack a dozen or so leaves at a time and then roll tightly, jelly roll-fashion. Place on a cutting board and cut each roll crosswise into 1/2-inch strips. Continue rolling and cutting this way until all the greens are cut.

✹ Rinse the greens at least 4 or 5 times in a large basin of cold water, swishing to remove any sand or dirt. Drain well.

✹ Heat a scant 2 tablespoons or so of the oil in a large heavy pot. Place about 1/3 of the greens at a time in the pot and sauté, stirring, for 5 or 6 minutes, or until the greens are wilted. Remove from the pot.

✹ Add the remaining greens and 1 tablespoon oil and sauté in the same way. When all the greens are sautéed, add the remaining oil to the pot, stir in the onion and garlic, and sauté for 4 or 5 minutes, or until the onion is tender. Return the greens to the pot.

✹ Add the chicken broth, salt and pepper. Cover and cook over low heat for 30 minutes or until the greens are tender. Serve hot.

SERVES 6

RICH IN **vitamins** AND **minerals**, COLLARD GREENS ARE A **good** ADDITION TO ANY DINNER. WHEN PURCHASED, THEY STILL MAY HAVE SOME SAND AND GRIT IN THE **leaves**; BE SURE TO WASH THEM VERY **well** BEFORE COOKING.

Grilled Wild Mushrooms with Teriyaki Dressing

NINA SIMONDS/REPRINTED FROM *A SPOONFUL OF GINGER* (KNOPF)

SERVES 6

HERE MUSHROOMS ARE

DRENCHED IN A simple

SOY dressing, THEN

SEARED OVER A HOT FIRE.

THEIR SMOKY, juicy

FLAVOR IS LIKE THAT OF

GRILLED MEAT.

$^{1}/_{2}$ pound medium to large fresh shiitake
mushrooms (about 12)
$^{1}/_{2}$ pound fresh oyster, cépe, maitake or
other wild mushrooms (about 12)
10 to 12 whole green onions, trimmed
and cut into $1^{1}/_{2}$-inch lengths
About 16 to 20 bamboo skewers, soaked
in cold water for 1 hour

Teriyaki Dressing
$^{1}/_{2}$ cup soy sauce
$^{1}/_{3}$ cup rice wine or sake
3 tablespoons water
2 tablespoons sugar
1 tablespoon toasted sesame oil
$1^{1}/_{2}$ tablespoons minced fresh ginger

✴ Trim the stem ends of the mushrooms, rinse lightly and drain thoroughly. If the mushroom caps are large, cut them in half. Thread 2 mushrooms and 3 green onion sections alternately onto each skewer, starting and ending with the green onions. Arrange the skewered vegetables on a baking sheet.

✴ Combine the teriyaki dressing ingredients in a saucepan. Heat until boiling, stirring to dissolve the sugar. Use $^{1}/_{3}$ of the dressing to liberally brush the mushrooms and green onions. Pour the remaining $^{2}/_{3}$ into a serving bowl.

✴ Prepare a medium-low fire for grilling and place the grill grate 3 to 4 inches from the heat. Arrange the skewered mushrooms and green onions on the grill and cook, turning frequently, for about 4 or 5 minutes, or until golden brown and slightly crisp at the edges.

✴ Arrange the vegetables on a serving platter. Serve with the warm teriyaki dressing for dipping.

Grilled Wild Mushrooms with
Teriyaki Dressing, and Grilled Ginger
Teriyaki Tuna (recipe page 81)

Grilled Dilled Tomatoes

STEVEN RAICHLEN/REPRINTED FROM *THE BARBECUE BIBLE* **(WORKMAN)**

8 fresh, ripe tomatoes or plum tomatoes
2 tablespoons olive oil

Salt and freshly ground black pepper
    to taste
2 tablespoons chopped fresh dill

✱ Preheat the grill to high.

✱ Thread the tomatoes on metal skewers, brush with oil, and season with salt and pepper.

✱ When ready to cook, place the skewers on the hot grate and grill the tomatoes, turning as necessary, until the skins are charred and blistered and the flesh inside is hot and soft, about 8 to 12 minutes total. Ease the tomatoes off the skewers with a fork, then sprinkle the tomatoes with dill and serve immediately.

Grilled Corn with Shadon Beni Butter

STEVEN RAICHLEN/REPRINTED FROM *THE BARBECUE BIBLE* **(WORKMAN)**

8 ears of corn (the larger and older,
    the better)
8 tablespoons (1 stick) salted butter, at
    room temperature

3 tablespoons finely chopped fresh
    culantro or cilantro
2 green onions, minced
1 clove garlic, minced
Freshly ground black pepper to taste

✱ Preheat the grill to high.

✱ Shuck the corn and set aside. Place the butter, herbs, green onions, garlic and pepper in a food processor and process until smooth. Transfer to a bowl. (Alternatively, if the herbs and garlic are minced really fine, you can stir them right into the butter in the bowl.)

✱ When ready to cook, oil the grill grate. Arrange the corn on the hot grate and grill, turning with tongs, until nicely browned all over, 8 to 12 minutes. As the corn cooks, brush it occasionally with the butter. Remove from the grill and brush once more with the butter. Serve immediately.

Grilled Dilled Tomatoes, Grilled Corn with Shadon Beni Butter, and Piri Piri Chicken (recipe page 92)

SERVES 4

USE SMALLISH TOMATOES (2½ TO 3 INCHES ACROSS) THAT ARE firm BUT RIPE. FLAT METAL skewers WORK BEST FOR HOLDING THE tomatoes, WHICH WOULD SLIP OFF A SLIM METAL SKEWER.

SERVES 8

SHADON BENI (LITERALLY "FALSE CILANTRO") IS A DARK-green, THUMB-SHAPED, SAWTOOTH-EDGED HERB WITH A taste SIMILAR TO CILANTRO. IT'S GENERALLY SOLD IN NORTH AMERICA BY ITS HISPANIC NAME, *CULANTRO*. (Look FOR IT IN HISPANIC AND WEST INDIAN MARKETS.) Cilantro MAKES AN EQUALLY DELICIOUS BUTTER.

Roasted Asparagus with Sesame Vinaigrette

NINA SIMONDS / REPRINTED FROM *SPOONFUL OF GINGER* (KNOPF)

SERVES 6

WHILE THIS PREPARATION IS UNKNOWN IN CHINA, THE sesame-soy VINAIGRETTE ADDS A WONDERFUL ASIAN flair TO FRESH ASPARAGUS.

2 pounds fresh asparagus, tough woody
   stems snapped off
2 teaspoons toasted sesame oil
2 teaspoons virgin olive oil
1/4 teaspoon salt

Sesame Vinaigrette
1/3 cup soy sauce
3 tablespoons clear rice vinegar
1/2 tablespoon toasted sesame oil
1 tablespoon sugar

2 tablespoons minced fresh Italian parsley
   (optional)

✳ Preheat the oven to 475°F. Rinse the asparagus stalks and drain on paper towels. Spread the stalks out on a baking sheet. Combine the sesame and olive oils and brush the asparagus with the oil, then sprinkle the salt over the stalks.

✳ Roast the asparagus for 10 to 12 minutes, or until they are tender when pierced with the tip of a knife. (Alternatively, you can steam the asparagus for 4 to 5 minutes until tender.) Arrange the asparagus on a serving plate.

✳ Mix together the sesame vinaigrette ingredients and drizzle over the asparagus. Sprinkle the minced parsley over the top, if desired. Serve hot or at room temperature.

Lime-Pickled Red Onions

BRUCE AIDELLS / REPRINTED FROM *THE COMPLETE MEAT COOKBOOK* (HOUGHTON MIFFLIN)

MAKES 1 CUP

TRY THESE zesty ONION SLICES IN TACOS, BURRITOS AND QUESADILLAS. THEY'RE great ON SANDWICHES OF ALL SORTS TOO, OR TO liven UP GRILLED FISH OR CHICKEN BREASTS.

1 large red onion, thinly sliced
1/4 cup fresh lime juice
1 tablespoon olive oil

1/2 teaspoon chopped fresh cilantro
1 teaspoon chopped fresh oregano, or
   1/2 teaspoon dried

✳ Mix all the ingredients together and let the onions marinate for at least 3 hours at room temperature. The onions will keep for up to 4 days, covered, in the refrigerator.

Vegetable Wreath

MARLENE SOROSKY / REPRINTED FROM *SEASON'S GREETINGS* (CHRONICLE)

1 large zucchini, ends trimmed
3 large red bell peppers
1 pound green beans, stem ends trimmed
1 large head broccoli, cut into florets
1 large head cauliflower, cut into florets

1 pound sugar snap or snow peas,
  trimmed
Salt and freshly ground black pepper
  to taste
Melted butter for drizzling
Lemon juice for drizzling

✴ With a serrated cutter or sharp knife, cut the zucchini into ½-inch diagonal slices. Cut 2 of the peppers in half, remove the seeds and cut into ½-inch strips.

✴ Bring 1 inch of salted water to a boil in a large Dutch oven or 12-inch skillet with a lid. Add the green beans, cover and steam for 1 minute. Top with the broccoli, cauliflower, peas and zucchini. Cover and steam over medium-high heat until tender-crisp, 5 to 6 minutes. Remove from the heat and drain.

✴ Meanwhile, place the pepper strips in a shallow microwave-safe dish with about ¼ inch of water. Cover with vented plastic wrap and microwave on high (100%) for 1 to 2 minutes, or until tender-crisp. Remove to a plate and cool to room temperature. (Alternatively, the peppers can be steamed or blanched in boiling water on top of the stove.) Cut the remaining pepper into a bow and microwave it in the same manner, until slightly wilted.

✴ As close to serving time as possible, arrange the vegetables in a wreath on a large round platter. Season as desired. Place the red pepper bow on top. If desired, reheat the vegetables in the microwave. Drizzle with butter and lemon juice.

SERVES 12

ENLIVEN YOUR HOLIDAY BUFFET WITH THIS festive VEGETABLE PRESENTATION. SHAPED LIKE A wreath, THE RED AND GREEN COLORS OF THE VEGETABLES BRING TO MIND holiday celebrations.

SERVES 4

THIS mixture OF

SEVERAL VEGETABLES,

FULL OF MANY TEXTURES

AND flavors, IS A

WONDERFUL SIDE DISH.

Harmonious Vegetable Stir-Fry

EILEEN YIN-FEI LO/REPRINTED FROM *THE CHINESE KITCHEN* (WILLIAM MORROW)

6 cups cold water
One 1/4-inch-thick slice fresh ginger,
   lightly smashed
10 ounces mung bean sprouts
1 1/2 teaspoons peanut oil

1/2 teaspoon salt
1 1/2 teaspoons minced garlic
3/4 cup 2-by-1/2-by-1/8-inch carrot slices
2/3 cup 1/4-inch-thick slices peeled and
   seeded cucumbers
1/2 teaspoon sesame oil

✳ Blanch the mung bean sprouts: Place the water and ginger in a pot, cover the pot and bring the water to a boil over high heat. Add the sprouts and cook for 5 minutes. Immediately turn off the heat and run cold water into the pot. Drain the sprouts and repeat the boiling and cooling process. Drain the sprouts well and discard the ginger. Set the sprouts aside.

✳ Heat a wok over high heat for 45 seconds. Add the peanut oil and spread out with a spatula. When a wisp of white smoke appears, add the salt and garlic. Stir-fry for 10 seconds, until the garlic's aroma is released. Add the carrots and stir-fry for 2 1/2 minutes, until they soften slightly. Add the cucumbers and stir-fry for 1 minute, until softened. Add the blanched sprouts and stir-fry for 10 seconds. Turn off the heat and continue to stir-fry for 10 seconds. Stir in the sesame oil and mix well. Transfer the vegetables to a heated dish and serve immediately.

Fava Bean Gratin

GERALD HIRIGOYEN/REPRINTED FROM *THE BASQUE KITCHEN* (HARPERCOLLINS)

6 pounds fresh fava beans in their pods (about 3 1/2 cups shelled and peeled beans)

3 tablespoons unsalted butter

2 large shallots, finely diced

1 1/2 teaspoons kosher salt

1/2 teaspoon freshly ground white pepper

3 tablespoons chopped fresh Italian parsley

2 tablespoons fine dry bread crumbs

3 tablespoons freshly grated sheep's milk cheese, such as Idiazabal

✳ Shell the fava beans.

✳ Fill a large saucepan ⅔ full of water and bring to a boil. Add the beans to the boiling water and cook just until tender, 2 to 3 minutes. Drain and immediately pinch off the skins from the beans with your fingers; set aside.

✳ Preheat the broiler.

✳ Warm the butter and shallots in a large skillet over medium heat, and sauté just until the shallots become translucent, 2 to 3 minutes. Add the fava beans, salt, pepper and parsley, and stir together gently. Continue to cook for 2 to 3 minutes, until the beans are hot throughout.

✳ Transfer the beans to a shallow ovenproof serving dish. Scatter the bread crumbs and cheese evenly over the top. Place under the broiler until the surface is lightly browned, about 3 minutes.

SERVES 4

WHEN favas COME INTO SEASON IN THE LATE SPRING AND EARLY SUMMER, INVITE SOME friends OVER FOR AN AFTERNOON OF GOOD CONVERSATION WHILE SHELLING AND SKINNING THE BEANS; THEN, MAKE THIS DISH AND serve IT WITH LAMB OR FISH. THE gratin COULD ALSO BE SERVED AS AN appetizer.

MAKES TWELVE
4-INCH PANCAKES

FOR THESE CLASSIC JEWISH
treats, THE COOKS AT
JUNIOR'S RESTAURANT IN
BROOKLYN, NEW YORK,
GRIND THE POTATOES WITH
AN OLD-FASHIONED HAND-
CRANKED MEAT GRINDER.
IF YOU DON'T HAVE ONE,
grate THEM BY HAND
ON A BOX GRATER, OR IN
A FOOD PROCESSOR USING
THE GRATING disk.

Homemade Potato Pancakes

ALAN ROSEN/FROM *WELCOME TO JUNIOR'S!* (WILLIAM MORROW)

2 pounds all-purpose boiling potatoes
1 cup grated onion
1/2 cup all-purpose flour
1 tablespoon baking powder
1 tablespoon sugar
1 tablespoon salt
1/2 teaspoon ground white pepper
2 extra-large eggs, beaten
3 tablespoons unsalted butter
1 tablespoon vegetable oil
Sour cream or applesauce for
    accompaniment

✱ Peel and grate or finely shred the potatoes (you need 4 cups of potatoes) and let them stand in ice water for 15 minutes.

✱ Fill a medium saucepan half-full with water and bring it to a boil over high heat. Drop in the drained potatoes and the onion and cook for 2 minutes. Pour the vegetables through a colander and squeeze out the excess water; pat dry on paper towels, then transfer to a large bowl.

✱ Mix the flour, baking powder, sugar, salt and pepper together in a cup, then toss with the potatoes and onions. Fold in the eggs just until the potatoes are coated. Do not overmix the batter at this stage, as this can make the pancakes tough and heavy.

✱ Heat the butter and oil in a large nonstick skillet over medium heat until the butter melts. For each cake, scoop about 1/3 cup of the batter and place in the hot pan, making 4-inch cakes about 1 inch apart. Fry the cakes until golden brown and crispy on both sides, about 6 minutes in all. Watch the heat closely so the skillet does not get too hot; you want the pancakes to fry just fast enough to turn a golden brown on the outside (no darker) and cook the potatoes on the inside. Serve the pancakes immediately with sour cream or applesauce.

NOTE: If you have some potato pancakes left over, slip them into self-sealing freezer bags and keep them in the freezer for up to 1 month. To serve, preheat the oven to 375°F. Place the frozen potato cakes directly on the middle oven rack and heat until hot and sizzling, about 8 minutes.

Longevity Noodles

EILEEN YIN-FEI LO/REPRINTED FROM *THE CHINESE KITCHEN* (WILLIAM MORROW)

10 cups cold water

5 ounces soybean sprouts, rinsed and drained

1 1/2 teaspoons salt

8 ounces egg noodles, prefried "longevity noodles"

1 tablespoon peanut oil

One 1/4-inch-thick slice fresh ginger, lightly smashed

4 ounces snow peas, strings removed

3 large fresh water chestnuts, peeled, cut into 1/8-inch-thick slices

Sauce

3 1/2 teaspoons light soy sauce

1/2 teaspoon sesame oil

1/4 cup chicken broth

✳ Place the water in a large pot, cover the pot and bring the water to a boil over high heat. Place the soybean sprouts in a mesh strainer and lower it into the boiling water for 15 seconds. Drain the sprouts and set aside.

✳ Add the salt to the pot and bring the water back to a boil. Add the noodles to the water, loosening them with chopsticks. Cook the noodles for 1 minute. Turn off the heat and run cold water into the pot to stop the boiling process. Bring the water back to a boil, cook the noodles for 1 more minute and cool again with cold water. Drain the noodles thoroughly, using chopsticks to loosen them. Set aside.

✳ Heat a wok over high heat for 45 seconds. Add the peanut oil and spread the oil out with a spatula. When a wisp of white smoke appears, add the ginger and stir-fry for 10 seconds. Add the snow peas and stir-fry for 1 minute, or until the snow peas turn bright green. Add the water chestnuts and stir-fry for 1 minute.

✳ In a small bowl or cup, stir the sauce ingredients together and pour into the wok. When the sauce comes to a boil, add the noodles and stir-fry briskly until all of the ingredients are mixed and the sauce is absorbed into the noodles, about 1 1/2 minutes. Turn off the heat and transfer the mixture to warm serving plates. Serve immediately.

SERVES 4

THIS IS A CLASSIC CHINESE celebration DISH, CONNOTING LONG-LIFE AT birthdays, ANNIVERSARIES AND NEW YEARS' BANQUETS.

LOOK FOR longevity NOODLES AND FRESH WATER CHESTNUTS IN AN Asian MARKET.

Grilled New Potatoes with a Garlicky Mustard Crust

W. PARK KERR / REPRINTED FROM *THE EL PASO CHILE COMPANY'S SIZZLIN' SUPPERS* **(WILLIAM MORROW)**

SERVES 6 TO 8

THE secret TO SUCCESS-
FULLY grilling THESE
POTATOES IS TO CUT THEM
INTO CHUNKS THAT ARE
big ENOUGH THAT THEY
DON'T FALL THROUGH THE
GRILL GRATE. SERVE THEM
WITH GRILLED SALMON
NIÇIOISE, PAGE 59, OR JUST
ABOUT ANYTHING.

2 pounds small new potatoes, scrubbed
1/2 cup Dijon-style mustard
1/4 cup olive oil
1 tablespoon fresh rosemary leaves, or
   1 teaspoon dried

1 teaspoon yellow mustard seeds
4 cloves garlic, crushed through a press
1/2 teaspoon salt
1/4 teaspoon freshly ground black pepper

✹ In a large pot of salted water, simmer the potatoes until just tender, about 20 minutes. Drain and rinse under cold water until cool enough to handle. Cut each potato in half.

✹ In a large bowl, whisk together the mustard, oil, rosemary, mustard seeds, garlic, salt and pepper. Add the potatoes and toss well to coat. Cover and let stand at room temperature for at least 15 minutes and up to 2 hours.

✹ Build a hot fire in an outdoor grill and let the coals burn until they are covered with white ash and you can hold your hand over the coals for 2 to 3 seconds. Oil the grill grate well to keep the potatoes from sticking. Cook, turning occasionally, until tender and crusty on all sides, 8 to 10 minutes. Use a large spatula to transfer the potatoes to a bowl.

NOTE: To serve the potatoes with the Grilled Salmon Salad Niçoise (page 59), let the salmon cook for 5 minutes, then place the potatoes around the salmon so they will be finished at the same time.

Grilled New Potatoes with a Garlicky Mustard Crust, and Grilled Salmon Salad Niçoise (recipe page 59)

Potatoes Baked in Milk and Cream

COLMAN ANDREWS/REPRINTED FROM *SAVEUR COOKS AUTHENTIC FRENCH* **(CHRONICLE)**

2 pounds russet potatoes, peeled and
  thinly sliced
1¹/₂ cups milk (or more if necessary)
1¹/₂ cups heavy cream

Salt and freshly ground black pepper
  to taste
Freshly grated nutmeg to taste

✱ Preheat the oven to 275°F. Arrange layers of slightly overlapping potato slices in an 8-cup gratin or baking dish. Mix together the milk and cream in a bowl, then pour the mixture over the potatoes to cover them completely (use a little more milk if needed). Bake for 1½ hours.

✱ Increase the oven heat to 400°F. Remove the pan from the oven and generously season the top of the potatoes with salt, pepper and nutmeg. Return the pan to the oven and bake until the potatoes are brown and bubbling, about 30 minutes more.

Sweet Potato Gratin

MARLENE SOROSKY

6 medium-sized sweet potatoes (about
  3¹/₂ pounds), peeled, ends trimmed
Salt and freshly ground black pepper
  to taste

1 jalapeño chile, minced
2 cups heavy cream

✱ Preheat the oven to 350°F. Lightly oil a 9-by-13-inch baking dish.

✱ Cut the sweet potatoes into ¼-inch-thick slices with a food processor or knife. Place a layer of potatoes in the dish and sprinkle with salt, pepper and minced jalapeño. Repeat the layering process until all the ingredients are used. Pour the cream over the top.

✱ Bake the dish, uncovered, for 45 minutes. If the top seems dry, baste it lightly with cream from around the edges. Continue to bake for 60 to 65 minutes, until the cream around the edges is very thick and the top is golden. Cut into squares to serve.

Potatoes Baked in Milk and Cream

CALLED *GRATIN DAUPHINOIS* IN ITS NATIVE FRANCE, THIS **rich** POTATO CASSEROLE IS SUPER-EASY TO MAKE. BE SURE TO **plan** AHEAD, HOWEVER; IT TAKES ABOUT 2 HOURS TO BAKE FOR A **luscious**, CREAMY INTERIOR AND A CRISP, GOLDEN **brown** EXTERIOR.

THOUGH IT MAY SEEM AN UNUSUAL INGREDIENT, JALAPEÑO ADDS A **zesty** **kick** TO THIS CASSEROLE, AND IS A **nice** FOIL TO THE **sweetness** OF THE POTATOES AND THE RICHNESS OF THE CREAM.

Potato "Gatto"

LYNNE ROSSETTO KASPER/REPRINTED FROM *THE ITALIAN COUNTRY TABLE* (SCRIBNER)

SERVES 6 TO 8

LYNNE'S COUNTRY-STYLE

ITALIAN casserole

FEATURES LAYERS OF POTA-

TOES, MEATS, VEGETABLES

AND cheese. BREAD

CRUMBS TOP THE DISH

BEFORE A LAST-MINUTE

flash IN THE OVEN FOR

A crispy TOPPING.

3 pounds yellow Finn or red-skinned
    potatoes
Extra-virgin olive oil
1 medium onion, cut into 1/4-inch dice
Salt and freshly ground black pepper
    to taste
1 large clove garlic, peeled
Three to four 1-inch-thick slices country
    bread, torn into bite-sized pieces
4 tablespoons (1/2 stick) unsalted butter

1 cup freshly grated Parmigiano-Reggiano
    cheese
1/3 cup milk
Five 1/8-inch-thick slices soppressatta
    or other good-tasting salami (about
    4 ounces), cut into 1/4-inch dice
1 1/3 cups tiny frozen peas, thawed
1/2 pound fresh mozzarella cheese in
    liquid, drained and sliced 1/4-inch thick

✴ Place the potatoes in a 4-quart pot, cover with water and simmer for 25 minutes, or until tender.

✴ While the potatoes cook, lightly coat a 10-inch skillet with olive oil and heat over medium-high heat. Add the onion and sauté quickly until golden, seasoning with salt and pepper. Transfer the onion to a bowl. Wipe out the skillet with paper towels and set aside.

✴ Turn on a food processor, drop in the garlic, then the bread, and process until the bread is in coarse crumbs (about ½-inch pieces). Coat the skillet again with oil. Add the bread and stir over medium heat, sprinkling with salt and pepper, about 5 minutes, or until pale gold. Turn out onto a sheet of foil and cool.

✴ Preheat the oven to 400°F. Oil an 8-inch square baking dish or pan.

✴ Slice the butter into a large bowl. Drain the potatoes, peel and add to the bowl. Mash the potatoes with a large fork, blending in the Parmigiano, milk and salt and pepper to taste. The potatoes should be lumpy. Fold in the salami and ½ of the peas. Spread ½ of the potato mixture in the baking dish. Top with the remaining peas and the onions, then the sliced mozzarella. Cover with the rest of the potato mixture. (At this point, you can cover and refrigerate the casserole overnight. Bring it to room temperature before baking.)

✴ Bake the casserole for about 30 minutes, or until it is hot. Top with the bread crumbs, pressing them into the potatoes a bit. Bake the casserole for another 10 minutes. Serve hot, cut into squares.

Mashed Potato Cake with Gruyère Cheese

MICHAEL ROBERTS/REPRINTED FROM *PARISIAN HOME COOKING* **(WILLIAM MORROW)**

4 large russet potatoes
6 tablespoons (3/4 stick) unsalted butter
1/4 cup dry bread crumbs
3 tablespoons finely chopped fresh parsley
3 tablespoons minced fresh chives
1 medium onion, finely chopped, or
 1 large leek, white part only, thinly
 sliced and washed well

1 3/4 cups milk
Pinch of freshly grated nutmeg
2 large eggs
2 large egg yolks
3/4 cup grated Gruyère cheese
3/4 teaspoon salt
Freshly ground black pepper to taste

✳ Preheat the oven to 400°F. Bake the potatoes until tender, about 1 hour. Remove from the oven and scoop the flesh into a mixing bowl. Reduce the oven temperature to 375°F.

✳ Meanwhile, generously butter a 2-quart ring mold (7 or 8 inches in diameter) with 1 tablespoon of the butter. Mix the bread crumbs, parsley and chives together in a small bowl and sprinkle evenly over the inside of the mold. Set the mold aside.

✳ Melt the remaining 5 tablespoons butter in a small saucepan. Add the onion and sauté until soft but not browned, about 3 minutes. Add the milk and nutmeg. Pour this mixture into the potatoes, then add the eggs and yolks. Using a large fork, lightly mash the potatoes, incorporating the milk and eggs, but leaving many lumps. Mix in the cheese. Season with the salt and pepper.

✳ Scoop the potato mixture evenly into the prepared mold. Place in the oven and bake for 45 minutes, or until the sides turn golden and begin to pull away from the mold. Remove from the oven, run a knife around the potatoes to loosen the cake from the mold, and turn it out onto a serving plate. Serve immediately, cut into wedges.

Savannah Red Rice

JOYCE WHITE / REPRINTED FROM *SOUL FOOD* (HARPERCOLLINS)

4 to 5 bacon strips	2 cups finely chopped tomatoes
1 onion	$1/2$ cup water
1 green or red bell pepper	$3/4$ teaspoon salt
2 tablespoons vegetable oil	$1/4$ teaspoon freshly ground black pepper
1 cup long-grain white rice	$1/2$ teaspoon hot pepper sauce

✳ Preheat the oven to 350°F. Oil a 2-quart ovenproof baking dish and set aside.

✳ In a medium skillet, fry the bacon until it is very brown and crisp; remove from the pan and set aside.

✳ Chop the onion and core and dice the green or red pepper.

✳ Drain off the bacon fat from the pan and discard. Add the oil to the pan. Stir in the onion and pepper and sauté over medium-low heat for 4 to 5 minutes, or until the vegetables are translucent and tender.

✳ Remove the pan from the heat and stir in the rice, tomatoes, water, salt, black pepper and hot pepper sauce. Spoon the rice mixture into the baking dish. Crumble the bacon and sprinkle it over the rice. Cover the pan tightly with a lid or aluminum foil.

✳ Place the dish on the lower shelf of the oven and bake for 45 to 50 minutes, or until the rice is tender, stirring two or three times during baking. Serve hot.

SERVES 4

TOMATOES AND A DASH OF HOT PEPPER sauce STAIN WHITE RICE A RED COLOR IN THE style OF SAVANNAH, GEORGIA. FOR MORE RED color AND SLIGHTLY SWEETER TASTE, USE RED BELL PEPPERS. FOR A lively COLOR CONTRAST, CHOOSE THE GREEN VARIETY.

Rice Croquettes with Currant Jelly

MARION CUNNINGHAM/REPRINTED FROM *THE ORIGINAL BOSTON COOKING-SCHOOL COOK BOOK* **(HUGH LAUTER LEVIN)**

½ cup rice	1 tablespoon butter
½ cup boiling water	Vegetable oil for frying
½ teaspoon salt	Dried bread crumbs
1 cup milk, scalded	Beaten eggs
2 egg yolks	Currant jelly

✳ Wash the rice and add it to the water in a saucepan with the salt. Cover the pan and steam until the rice has absorbed all of the water, about 15 to 18 minutes. Add the milk, stir lightly with a fork, cover and steam until the rice is soft, about 5 to 10 minutes. Remove the pan from the heat and stir in the egg yolks and the butter. Spread the rice mixture out on a shallow plate to cool.

✳ In a large, high-sided skillet, heat about 2 inches of the oil until it reaches 350°F.

✳ Shape the rice mixture into 6 balls, roll them in the bread crumbs and form them into nest shapes. Dip the nests into egg and again into the bread crumbs. Carefully fry the nests in the hot oil until golden brown; drain on paper towels and keep warm in a low oven. To serve, place a small amount of the jelly in the center of each croquette. Arrange the croquettes on a plate. Serve hot.

SOUPS, SALADS & SMALL DISHES

Grilled Gazpacho

STEVEN RAICHLEN/REPRINTED FROM *THE BARBECUE BIBLE* **(WORKMAN)**

4 green onions

2 cloves garlic

1 medium-sized red onion, root ends left
on, quartered

$1/3$ cup extra-virgin olive oil

Two $3/4$-inch slices country-style white
bread or French bread

5 fresh, ripe, medium-sized tomatoes
(about $2 1/2$ pounds)

1 medium-sized red bell pepper

1 medium-sized green bell pepper

1 medium cucumber, peeled

$1/4$ cup mixed chopped fresh herbs, such
as basil, oregano, tarragon and/or
Italian parsley

2 tablespoons red wine vinegar, or more
to taste

$1/2$ to 1 cup cold water, or more as needed

Salt and freshly ground black pepper
to taste

✱ Preheat the grill to high.

✱ Finely chop the green parts of the green onions and set aside for garnish. Thread the
white parts of the green onions onto a skewer and add the garlic cloves. Thread the onion
quarters on a second skewer. Lightly brush the green onion whites, garlic and onions with
about 1 tablespoon of the oil.

✱ When ready to cook, oil the grill grate. Place the skewers on the hot grate and grill,
turning with tongs, until the vegetables are nicely browned, 4 to 8 minutes in all. Transfer to a plate to cool. Add the bread slices to the grate and grill until darkly toasted, 1 to
2 minutes per side. Set aside. Grill the tomatoes and bell peppers until the skins are
nicely charred, about 8 to 12 minutes in all for the tomatoes, 16 to 20 minutes for the
peppers. Transfer to a platter to cool. Using a paring knife, scrape the charred skins off
the tomatoes, onions and peppers (don't worry about removing every last bit). Core and
seed the peppers.

✱ Cut the green onion whites, garlic, onions, bread, tomatoes, bell peppers and cucumber
into 1-inch pieces. Place the pieces in a blender, adding the tomatoes first, along with the
herbs, 2 tablespoons vinegar and the remaining oil. Process to a smooth puree. Thin the
gazpacho to pourable consistency with water as needed and season with salt and pepper.

✱ The gazpacho can be served now, but it will taste even better if you chill it for an hour
or so to allow the flavors to blend. Just before serving, correct the seasoning, adding salt
or vinegar as necessary. To serve, ladle the gazpacho into bowls and sprinkle with the
chopped green onions.

SERVES 8

GRILLING ADDS A SMOKY
DIMENSION TO GAZPACHO,
WHICH transforms
THIS WARM-WEATHER SOUP
FROM THE REALM OF
refreshing TO UNFOR-
GETTABLE. IF USING A FOOD
PROCESSOR, puree THE
VEGETABLES FIRST, THEN
ADD THE LIQUIDS.

Chipotle Cheese Soup

BILL HUFNAGLE/REPRINTED FROM *BIKER BILLY'S FREEWAY-A-FIRE* (WILLIAM MORROW)

1 large broccoli stalk with florets
3 tablespoons butter
1/2 teaspoon celery seeds
2 cups baby carrots, quartered
1 medium onion, diced
1 to 2 chipotle chiles packed in adobo
    sauce, or to taste, minced, plus
    1 tablespoon adobo sauce
5 cups water
2 tablespoons chopped garlic

1 tablespoon dried parsley
1 teaspoon ground savory
1 teaspoon salt
1 teaspoon freshly ground black pepper
1 red bell pepper, cored, seeded and diced
1 cup milk
1 pound Velveeta cheese, cut into 1/2-inch
    chunks
1 tablespoon all-purpose flour

✱ Trim the broccoli, remove the florets, coarsely chop them and set aside. Thinly slice the stalk.

✱ Melt 2 tablespoons of the butter in a medium skillet over medium heat. Add the sliced broccoli stalk, celery seeds, carrots and onion. Cook until the onion is translucent, about 6 to 8 minutes.

✱ Transfer the cooked vegetables to a large soup pot set over high heat. Add the chipotle chiles, water, garlic, parsley, savory, salt and pepper and bring to a boil. Reduce the heat to medium, cover and simmer for 45 minutes, stirring often.

✱ Add the broccoli florets and bell pepper and stir well. Reduce the heat to low and simmer for 15 minutes, stirring often.

✱ Add the milk and Velveeta cheese and stir until the cheese melts. Reduce the heat to very low and simmer, stirring often, while you prepare the roux.

✱ In a small saucepan, melt the remaining 1 tablespoon butter over low heat. Add the flour and stir well. Continue to stir until the flour is a very light brown, 2 to 3 minutes. Add the adobo sauce and 2 cups of liquid from the soup and mix thoroughly with a wire whisk. Transfer the mixture to the soup and stir until well blended. Simmer, stirring often, until the soup thickens, 5 minutes. Serve immediately.

Tuscan Creamy Sweet Pepper Soup

JAMES MCNAIR/REPRINTED FROM *JAMES MCNAIR'S FAVORITES* (CHRONICLE)

4 large red or yellow bell peppers
2 tablespoons unsalted butter
1 cup chopped yellow onion
1 large baking potato (about 8 ounces),
  peeled and chopped
1 quart vegetable or low-sodium chicken
  broth, plus more if needed
2 cups water, plus more if needed

2 sprigs fresh thyme
2 bay leaves
Salt and freshly ground white pepper
  to taste
Extra-virgin olive oil for serving (optional)
Freshly grated Parmigiano-Reggiano
  cheese for serving

✳ To roast the peppers, place the peppers directly on a gas flame or under the broiler. Cook, turning with tongs, until the skins of the peppers are charred on all sides. Transfer the peppers to a bowl, cover, and let stand until cool enough to handle. With your hands or a paring knife, remove the charred skins from the peppers. Cut off the tops and discard the seeds and ribs. Chop the peppers coarsely and set aside.

✳ In a large saucepan, melt the butter over medium-high heat. Add the onion and sauté until soft but not browned, about 5 minutes. Add the potato, broth and water. Increase the heat to high, bring to a boil and cook for 15 minutes.

✳ Reduce the heat to achieve a simmer. Enclose the thyme and bay leaves in a small square of cheesecloth, tie with cotton string to form a bag and add to the simmering soup. Add the chopped peppers and simmer until the potatoes are falling apart and creamy, about 45 minutes longer; add more broth or water if the soup becomes too thick.

✳ Discard the bag of herbs. Working in batches if necessary, transfer the soup to a food processor or blender and puree until smooth. Season to taste with salt and pepper. (At this point, the soup can be cooled completely, then covered and refrigerated for up to 2 days. Slowly reheat before serving.)

✳ To serve, pour the soup into a clean pot and heat over low heat. Ladle the hot soup into warmed bowls, drizzle with olive oil, if using, and sprinkle with cheese.

SERVES 4

FOR AN attractive PRESENTATION, MAKE TWO BATCHES OF THIS CREAMY— YET CREAMLESS—soup, ONE WITH red PEPPERS AND THE OTHER WITH yellow PEPPERS. LADLE ONE SOUP INTO WARMED BOWLS TO FILL HALFWAY, THEN ladle THE SECOND SOUP INTO THE CENTER OF THE FIRST soup. DRAW A WOODEN SKEWER THROUGH THE SURFACE TO create AN INTEREST-ING PATTERN.

Citrus Caesar Dressing

MARLENE SOROSKY/REPRINTED FROM *ENTERTAINING ON THE RUN* (WILLIAM MORROW)

MARLENE SOROSKY/REPRINTED FROM *ENTERTAINING ON THE RUN* (WILLIAM MORROW)

5 tablespoons fresh lemon juice
6 to 8 tablespoons olive oil
3 tablespoons orange juice
2 teaspoons Worcestershire sauce

2 cloves garlic, minced
2 teaspoons dry mustard
2 teaspoons anchovy paste
Freshly ground black pepper to taste

✳ In a small bowl or wide-mouthed jar, mix the lemon juice, 6 tablespoons of the oil, orange juice, Worcestershire, garlic, mustard and anchovy paste. Taste and, if desired, add the remaining oil. Add the pepper. The dressing can be refrigerated, tightly covered, for up to 2 days. Remove from the refrigerator at least 1 hour before using and stir well.

MAKES ABOUT 1 CUP

PRESENT THIS DRESSING IN A decorative CRUET FOR THE BEST EYE-APPEAL. USE IT TO enliven CRISP ROMAINE LEAVES WITH YOUR FAVORITE GARNISHES, SUCH AS CRISP FRIED BACON, piquant OLIVES AND NUTTY PARMESAN CHEESE.

Herb Vinegar

MARLENE SOROSKY/REPRINTED FROM *SEASON'S GREETINGS* (CHRONICLE)

2 cups good-quality white wine vinegar
1/2 cup chopped fresh herbs
4 clean glass bottles

3 to 4 cloves garlic (optional)
4 to 8 sprigs fresh herbs
4 whole red or green chile peppers
   (optional)

✳ Place the vinegar in a nonaluminum saucepan and bring to a boil. Divide the chopped herbs among the bottles. Add the garlic, if using. Pour the hot vinegar over, cover and place in a cool, dark location for 5 days, stirring once a day. Strain.

✳ Add the sprigs of fresh herbs and chile pepper, if using. Store tightly capped in a cool, dark location for 2 months, or refrigerate for longer storage.

MAKES 2 CUPS

ALMOST ANY fresh HERB OR COMBINATION OF HERBS WILL enhance THE FLAVOR OF VINEGAR. THE chile ADDS A zesty TASTE.

Grilled Salmon Salad Niçoise

W. PARK KERR / REPRINTED FROM *THE EL PASO CHILE COMPANY'S SIZZLIN' SUPPERS* **(WILLIAM MORROW)**

Lemon Mustard Vinaigrette
2 tablespoons red wine vinegar
2 tablespoons fresh lemon juice
2 tablespoons minced shallots
1 tablespoon Dijon-style mustard
Grated zest of 1 lemon
1 teaspoon sugar
$1/2$ teaspoon salt
$1/4$ teaspoon freshly ground black pepper
$3/4$ cup extra-virgin olive oil

One $3^1/_2$- to 4-pound salmon fillet in 1 piece
$1/3$ cup sour cream
$1/3$ cup Dijon-style mustard
2 tablespoons chopped fresh dill or green onion (green part only)
$1/2$ teaspoon freshly ground black pepper
10 cups mesclun or other mixed salad greens
Grilled New Potatoes with a Garlicky Mustard Crust (see page 42)
2 cups cherry tomatoes, preferably both yellow and red

✳ To make the vinaigrette, whisk together all of the ingredients, except the oil, in a medium bowl. Gradually whisk in the oil until the vinaigrette thickens. Set aside.

✳ Using a pair of tweezers, feel over the cut surface of the salmon and remove any small bones. (Sterilize the tweezers first by holding over an open flame for a few seconds.)

✳ In a small bowl, mix the sour cream, mustard, dill and pepper.

✳ Build a charcoal fire in an outdoor grill and let the coals burn until covered with white ash. You should be able to hold your hand over the coals at grate level for 3 to 4 seconds. (Or preheat a gas grill to high, then adjust to medium.) Oil the grilling grate well to discourage the salmon skin from sticking. Spread the mustard mixture over the cut surface of the salmon fillet. Place the salmon skin side-down and cover the grill. Grill the salmon until the skin is crisp and blackened and the flesh looks barely opaque when prodded with a knife in the thickest part, about 15 to 20 minutes.

✳ Place the mesclun on a large platter and toss with the dressing. Using 2 large spatulas, transfer the salmon to the platter. Spoon the potatoes around the salmon. Sprinkle with the cherry tomatoes.

✳ To serve, cut the salmon vertically into portions, transfer to dinner plates, and serve with a heap of salad and potatoes on the side.

SERVES 8

COOKING THE SALMON THIS WAY creates A crisp, BLACKENED SKIN. THE TOP OF THE SALMON FILLET IS SPREAD WITH AN unusual SOUR CREAM AND MUSTARD glaze TO HELP KEEP THE FISH FROM DRYING OUT.

Warm Cucumber and Smoked Salmon Salad with Five-Grain Croutons

JIM COLEMAN/REPRINTED FROM *THE RITTENHOUSE COOKBOOK* (TEN SPEED)

Croutons
Two 1/4-inch-thick slices hearty 5-grain
  bread

Salad
1 teaspoon olive oil
1 English cucumber (about 12 ounces),
  peeled, seeded and cut into julienne

1/2 small red onion, cut into julienne
1 1/2 tablespoons unseasoned rice vinegar
2 tablespoons low-sodium chicken broth
Freshly ground white pepper to taste
1 tablespoon chopped fresh dill
12 thin slices smoked salmon (about
  6 ounces)
4 sprigs dill, for garnish

✷ To prepare the croutons, trim the crust from the slices and cut in half. Cut each half diagonally to form 2 triangles, giving you a total of 8 triangles. Toast the triangles lightly on each side under the broiler. Set aside.

✷ To prepare the salad, heat the olive oil in a skillet. Add the cucumber to the hot pan and sauté over high heat for 2 to 3 minutes, stirring constantly to avoid burning. Add the onion and continue sautéing the cucumber and onion for 2 to 3 minutes longer, or until translucent. Add the vinegar and broth and continue cooking until almost all of the liquid has evaporated. Remove from the heat and stir in the pepper and dill. Set aside.

✷ Spoon a mound of the cucumber salad in the center of each plate. Roll the salmon slices into cylinders and arrange 3 on each plate positioned at 4 o'clock, 8 o'clock, and 12 o'clock. Garnish with the dill and arrange 2 croutons on the sides of each plate.

Rainbow Salad with Spicy Peanut Dressing

NINA SIMONDS / REPRINTED FROM *A SPOONFUL OF GINGER* (KNOPF)

1 pound firm tofu, cut into 1/2-inch slabs

1/2 pound spinach or egg fettuccine

1 teaspoon toasted sesame oil

2 cups grated carrots

1 1/2 cups grated, peeled and seeded cucumbers

1 1/2 cups bean sprouts, rinsed and drained

1 red bell pepper, cored, seeded and cut into julienne

1 yellow bell pepper, cored, seeded and cut into julienne

Spicy Peanut Dressing

2 tablespoons minced fresh ginger

1/2 tablespoon minced garlic

1 teaspoon hot chile paste, or more to taste

1/2 cup smooth peanut butter, plus more if needed

1/4 cup soy sauce

3 1/2 tablespoons sugar

3 1/2 tablespoons Chinese black vinegar or Worcestershire sauce

3 tablespoons toasted sesame oil

5 tablespoons water or chicken broth, plus more if needed

SERVES 6

THIS DRESSING IS ONE OF NINA'S MOST REQUESTED recipes. IN ADDITION TO THIS salad, YOU CAN SERVE IT WITH ANY combination OF SHREDDED VEGETABLES. COOKED NOODLES add SUBSTANCE TO THE DISH.

✱ Wrap the tofu slabs in paper towels or a cotton towel, and place a heavy weight, such as a cast-iron skillet, on top. Let stand for 30 minutes to press out the excess water, then cut the tofu into matchstick-sized shreds about 2 inches long.

✱ Bring 3 quarts water to a boil, add the fettuccine, and cook until just tender. Drain in a colander, toss with the sesame oil and arrange on a platter.

✱ Arrange the carrots, cucumbers, bean sprouts, and red and yellow pepper strips in mounds or separate concentric circles on the serving platter with the noodles.

✱ To prepare the spicy peanut dressing, chop the ginger and garlic until fine in a food processor or a blender. Add the remaining ingredients in descending order, ending with the water or chicken broth. Process until smooth. The dressing should have the consistency of heavy cream. If it is too thick, add more water or broth; if too thin, add more peanut butter. Pour the dressing into a serving container, and offer the vegetables and dressing to each diner to mix as desired.

Shepherd's Salad

LYNNE ROSSETTO KASPER/REPRINTED FROM *THE ITALIAN COUNTRY TABLE* **(SCRIBNER)**

Dressing

3 tablespoons robust extra-virgin olive oil
1 thin slice mild coppa, soppressata or hard salami, cut into thin strips
1/2 medium to large red onion, cut into 1/2-inch dice
One 4-inch sprig fresh rosemary
6 large fresh sage leaves
4 large cloves garlic, minced
Pinch of crushed red pepper flakes
1/2 cup red wine vinegar, plus more as needed
2 cups chicken broth
Salt and freshly ground black pepper to taste

1 medium-sized red onion, sliced into thin rings
1 large head Bibb lettuce (preferably red)
1/2 large head romaine lettuce
3 to 4 cups mixed wild greens, or 1 small head curly endive
2 small inner stalks celery with leaves, cut on the diagonal into thin slices
1 small bulb fennel, cut into thin strips
6 thin slices mild coppa, soppressata or hard salami, cut into thin strips
1/4 pound Italian or American sheep cheese or Asiago cheese, cut into strips
2 cups cooked cannellini, borlotti or organic pinto beans, or one 15-ounce can beans
Salt and freshly ground black pepper

✻ To make the dressing, heat the oil in a 1-quart saucepan over medium-high heat. Add the salami, onion, rosemary and sage and sauté until the onion colors. Add the garlic and pepper flakes and stir for a few seconds, then add the vinegar. Boil for 4 minutes. Stir in 1 cup of the broth and boil until nearly all evaporated. Add the remaining broth and boil for 2 minutes. Taste and season with salt and pepper. Cover the pan and set aside until needed, up to 2 hours.

✻ Meanwhile, immerse the onion in ice water and refrigerate about 45 minutes. Drain.

✻ Wash and thoroughly dry the greens, setting aside any bruised or coarse leaves for other dishes. Arrange the greens on a large platter, contrasting the colors and shapes. Scatter the celery over the salad and tuck clusters of the fennel strips into it. If necessary, the salad can be covered and chilled for up to 2 hours.

✻ Shortly before serving, cluster the salami strips into 7 to 9 bundles, tucking them in here and there in the salad. Do the same with the drained onions and with the cheese strips. Nest large spoonfuls of the beans in several of the lettuce leaves. Sprinkle the salad lightly with salt and pepper.

✻ Bring the dressing to a boil. Taste for seasoning again, this time checking if it needs a tablespoon or so of vinegar. Present it in a deep bowl, and spoon it over the salad just before serving.

Nice-Style Stuffed Vegetables

COLMAN ANDREWS/REPRINTED FROM *SAVEUR COOKS AUTHENTIC FRENCH* (CHRONICLE)

3 small eggplants
6 small green or red bell peppers
1/2 cup extra-virgin olive oil
3 small yellow onions
3 zucchini
3 medium tomatoes
1/4 pound lean salt pork, diced
1/2 pound ground lamb
1/2 cup cooked rice

1/2 cup finely chopped fresh Italian parsley
2 cloves garlic, minced
Salt and freshly ground black pepper
   to taste
2 eggs, lightly beaten
1/2 cup finely grated Parmigiano-Reggiano
   cheese
1/2 cup fresh bread crumbs
1 bunch fresh thyme

SERVES 6

PREPARED IN THE STYLE OF NICE, WITH ITS lusty SUN-DRENCHED FLAVORS, THESE MEAT- AND RICE-STUFFED VEGETABLES MAKE A delightful LIGHT ENTRÉE OR SIDE DISH.

✳ Preheat the oven to 350°F.

✳ Cut the eggplants in half lengthwise. Cut the tops from the peppers, then core and seed them. Place the eggplants and peppers on an oiled baking sheet and brush lightly with oil. Bake for 30 minutes, then remove the vegetables from the oven and set aside to cool. When the eggplants are cool enough to handle, scoop out the pulp, leaving a shell about 1/2-inch thick. Chop the pulp finely and set aside in a large bowl.

✳ Heat a large pot of salted water over medium heat. Add the onions and zucchini and simmer for about 10 minutes. Drain and set aside to cool.

✳ Halve the onions crosswise and remove the centers, leaving a shell of about 3 outer layers. Halve the zucchini lengthwise and scoop out the pulp, leaving a shell about 1/2-inch thick. Halve the tomatoes crosswise, then squeeze out and discard the seeds and juice. Scoop the pulp from the tomatoes, finely chop, and add to the eggplant pulp. Finely chop the onion centers and zucchini pulp and add them to the eggplant mixture as well.

✳ Increase the oven temperature to 375°F. Heat 2 tablespoons of the oil in a large skillet over low heat. Stir in the vegetable mixture, salt pork, lamb, rice, parsley and garlic. Season to taste with salt and pepper Cook for about 15 minutes, stirring occasionally. Remove from the heat, cool slightly, then stir in the eggs.

✳ Fill the vegetable shells with the filling, taking care not to pack the filling too tightly. Top the filled shells with the Parmigiano and bread crumbs, drizzle with the remaining olive oil and bake for 30 minutes on an oiled baking sheet. Serve garnished with fresh thyme sprigs.

Smooth Tomato Sauce

ARTHUR SCHWARTZ/REPRINTED FROM *NAPLES AT TABLE* **(HARPERCOLLINS)**

2 tablespoons extra-virgin olive oil
1 small onion, finely chopped, or 1 large
   clove garlic, lightly smashed
One 28-ounce can plum tomatoes,
   drained of the can juices (*see note*)

¹/₂ teaspoon salt
Crushed red pepper flakes or freshly
   ground black pepper to taste
A few leaves of fresh basil or Italian parsley

✳ In a 1½- to 2-quart saucepan, combine the oil and onion and sauté over medium heat until the onion is tender and golden, 8 to 10 minutes. Or, over medium-low heat, combine the oil and the garlic. Cook the garlic, pressing it into the oil a couple of times to release its flavor, until it *barely* begins to color on both sides. Remove the garlic.

✳ With a food mill, puree the tomatoes directly into the saucepan and stir well. Add the salt and pepper flakes or pepper. Increase the heat slightly and bring to a brisk simmer. Adjusting the heat as the sauce cooks down, and stirring frequently, simmer briskly for about 12 minutes, until the sauce has thickened and reduced.

✳ Season the sauce with herbs according to the recipe you are preparing. For the most basic spaghetti sauce, add a few torn basil leaves or a tablespoon of finely cut parsley to the sauce while it is simmering, then add a little more of either at the very end of cooking.

VARIATION: Sometimes you will want a chunky sauce, not a smooth puree. Instead of pushing the tomatoes through a food mill, turn the whole can of tomatoes, drained or not, into the pot with the oil. Using the side of a wooden spoon, a wooden fork, or an old-fashioned American potato masher, break up the tomatoes as desired, then proceed as above.

NOTE: The easiest way to drain the tomatoes is to open the can but not remove the lid, then use the lid to hold back the tomatoes while the juices run into a cup or bowl.

**MAKES ABOUT 2 CUPS,
SERVES 4 WITH PASTA**

IT'S WORTH YOUR WHILE TO SEEK A high-quality BRAND OF BOTTLED OR CANNED TOMATOES, PREFERABLY ITALIAN, TO USE AS YOUR pantry STAPLE. SHOP FOR THEM IN A STORE THAT HAS HIGH VOLUME TO ENSURE A fresh PRODUCT. ACCORDING TO ARTHUR, ALL PROCESSED tomatoes SHOULD BE USED WITHIN 6 MONTHS OF PACKAGING.

Simple Veal Pasta Sauce

MARCELLA HAZAN/REPRINTED FROM *MARCELLA CUCINA* **(HARPERCOLLINS)**

3/4 pound fresh, ripe tomatoes, or 1 cup
   canned imported Italian plum tomatoes,
   chopped and drained of juice
3 tablespoons butter
1 tablespoon vegetable oil
1/4 cup chopped onion

1/2 pound ground veal
Salt and freshly ground black pepper
   to taste
1 pound pasta of your choice
1/4 cup freshly grated Parmigiano-Reggiano
   cheese

✳ If you are using fresh tomatoes, peel them by dipping them into boiling water for 1 minute, then peel off their skins. Halve the tomatoes, scoop out their seeds without squeezing and chop up coarsely.

✳ Place 2 tablespoons of the butter and the vegetable oil in a small saucepan over medium-high heat. Cook the onion, stirring from time to time, until it becomes colored a pale gold.

✳ Add the ground veal and turn it over several times, using a wooden spoon to brown it all over.

✳ Add the cut-up tomato, salt and several grindings of pepper, and with your wooden spoon turn over all ingredients two or three times. Cook at a steady but gentle simmer for 15 to 20 minutes.

✳ Cook and drain the pasta and toss it immediately and thoroughly with the sauce, swirling into it the remaining tablespoon of butter and the grated Parmigiano.

DO AHEAD TIPS: The sauce can be cooked a day in advance and refrigerated in a tightly sealed container. When reheating, add a tablespoon of water, bring to a gentle simmer, stir occasionally and cook until hot throughout.

SERVES 4 TO 6

THE ideal CARRIER FOR THIS SIMPLE MEAT SAUCE IS A HOMEMADE noodle, SUCH AS FETTUCCINE. A DRY PASTA IN A SHORT tubular SHAPE SUCH AS PENNE WORKS WELL, TOO.

Goat Cheese, Chive and Chile Pepper Sauce for Pasta

MARCELLA HAZAN/REPRINTED FROM *MARCELLA CUCINA* (HARPERCOLLINS)

6 ounces creamy goat cheese
1/4 cup extra-virgin olive oil
2 tablespoons chopped fresh chives

1/4 teaspoon chopped chile pepper, or
   to taste
Salt to taste
1 pound of pasta of your choice

✳ In a small bowl, combine the cheese, oil, chives, chile and salt and mix with a fork until smoothly and thoroughly combined.

✳ Cook the pasta and drain it, pouring some of the water into a serving bowl. Swirl the water around the bowl to warm it, then pour out all but a tablespoon of the water. The water will help the sauce, which is rather dry, coat the pasta more uniformly.

✳ Immediately place the drained pasta in the bowl, add the goat cheese mixture, toss thoroughly to spread the sauce and coat the pasta strands well and serve at once. No additional cheese is required.

SERVES 4 TO 6

THE FIRM bite AND COM-
PACT TEXTURE OF BOXED
dry PASTA ARE JUST WHAT
YOU WANT WITH THIS GOAT
CHEESE SAUCE. THE MOST
desirable SHAPE HERE
WOULD BE spaghettini
(THIN SPAGHETTI).

Baked Ziti

ARTHUR SCHWARTZ/REPRINTED FROM *NAPLES AT TABLE* (HARPERCOLLINS)

1 pound ziti
2 1/2 to 3 cups tomato sauce
1 cup whole-milk ricotta cheese
8 ounces mozzarella cheese, thinly sliced

About 10 basil leaves, torn into small
   pieces
1 cup grated Parmigiano-Reggiano or
   pecorino cheese, or a combination

✳ Preheat the oven to 350°F.

✳ Cook the ziti in boiling salted water according to the package directions, until it is almost tender enough to eat, about 2 minutes less than is indicated.

✳ While the pasta is cooking, blend 2 tablespoons of the tomato sauce into the ricotta in a large bowl. Spread about ¾ cup of the tomato sauce on the bottom of a 9-by-13-by-2-inch baking dish, or a round or oval dish of similar capacity (about 3½ quarts).

✳ When the ziti is done, drain it well, then toss it with the ricotta mixture. Spread ½ of the pasta in the baking dish. Evenly spoon over it ¾ cup of the tomato sauce. Cover with the sliced mozzarella, the basil and ½ cup of the Parmigiano. Top with the remaining pasta, tomato sauce and grated cheese. Bake for about 45 minutes, or until bubbling.

✳ Let the casserole cool for 10 minutes before cutting it into serving portions. Serve hot.

SERVES 4 TO 6

THIS VERSION OF BAKED
ziti IS LIGHTER THAN THE
USUAL ITALIAN-AMERICAN
STANDARD. IT'S A good
EXAMPLE OF HOW SOME
OF THE finesse OF THE
NEAPOLITAN KITCHEN HAS
BEEN LOST ON THIS SIDE
OF THE OCEAN.

Spaghetti Frittata

ARTHUR SCHWARTZ/REPRINTED FROM *NAPLES AT TABLE* (HARPERCOLLINS)

6 to 8 ounces linguine, spaghetti or other pasta, cooked and sauced or not sauced, leftover or freshly cooked, at room temperature
4 eggs, lightly beaten
Freshly ground black pepper to taste

½ cup freshly grated Parmigiano-Reggiano or pecorino cheese, or a combination (or more to taste)
1 tablespoon extra-virgin olive oil
5 ounces scamorza or several-days-old mozzarella cheese, sliced (optional)

✱ In a large mixing bowl, combine the pasta, beaten eggs, black pepper and grated cheese. Mix well.

✱ In a 9- to 10-inch nonstick skillet, heat the oil over medium heat and swirl it around to coat the bottom of the pan. Add ½ of the pasta and spread it evenly in the pan. Place the sliced cheese on top, if using, but don't place any cheese within ½ inch of the edge. Add the remaining pasta and spread it to make sure it covers the bottom pasta layer and the sliced cheese. Cook over medium heat for 5 to 8 minutes, or until the bottom browns.

✱ Place a plate on top of the pan and invert the frittata so that it falls onto the plate. Slip the frittata back into the skillet and cook the other side for another 5 to 8 minutes, until it browns. Serve hot, warm or at room temperature, cut into wedges.

VARIATIONS: Instead of scamorza or mozzarella, you can use any good melting cheese, such as Gouda, fontina, Gruyère, or Swiss (Emmenthaler).

In addition to, or instead of, the melting cheese, sprinkle a few extra tablespoons of grated cheese between the layers of pasta.

Add diced salami or diced, thinly sliced ham with the cheese.

SERVES 4 TO 8

IN THIS DISH, EGGS, CHEESE AND leftover SPAGHETTI ARE CLEVERLY COMBINED TO MAKE A delicious SPUR-OF-THE-MOMENT entrée, IN THE STYLE OF NAPLES, ITALY.

Upside-Down Tomato Tart

MICHAEL ROBERTS/REPRINTED FROM *PARISIAN HOME COOKING* **(WILLIAM MORROW)**

1/4 cup packed dark brown sugar	1/2 teaspoon freshly ground black pepper
1/2 cup red wine vinegar	3 sprigs fresh oregano, leaves only
12 firm, ripe Roma (plum) tomatoes (about	2 tablespoons extra-virgin olive oil
3 pounds)	1/2 recipe Savory Tart Dough (*recipe follows*)
2 teaspoons salt	Fresh basil sprigs for garnish

✳ Combine the sugar and vinegar in a saucepan, place over medium-high heat and boil the mixture until it turns dark and syrupy, about 3 minutes. Set aside.

✳ Cut out the tomato cores, quarter the tomatoes from tip to stem and gently squeeze out the seeds. Place the tomato quarters in a bowl, add the vinegar syrup, salt, pepper, oregano and olive oil and toss well.

✳ Arrange the tomatoes in a tight rose petal pattern in an 8-inch-round, 2-inch-deep nonstick baking dish; pour over any syrup remaining in the bowl. Place the dish in a cold oven and turn the oven to 375°F. Bake the tart for 1 hour.

✳ Roll out the dough into a 8-inch circle. Cover the tomatoes with the dough, return to the oven and bake for another 30 to 35 minutes, or until the crust is golden.

✳ Let the tart cool for 20 minutes, then invert it onto a plate. Garnish with fresh basil and serve at room temperature, cut into wedges.

Savory Tart Dough

1 1/2 cups pastry flour	3 tablespoons unsalted butter, chilled and
1/4 teaspoon salt	cut into 9 slices
1/4 teaspoon sugar	1 large egg yolk
	1 to 2 tablespoons ice water, if needed

✳ Combine the flour, salt and sugar in the bowl of a food processor or mixer. Add the butter and yolk. Pulse the food processor or run the mixer until the mixture just begins to hold together; it should resemble coarse meal. If the mixture seems too crumbly and won't hold together, add a tablespoon or two of water. Do not overwork the dough. Transfer the dough to a work surface and press it into a ball. Wrap in plastic wrap and refrigerate for 1 hour before using. (It can be frozen for up to one month.) *Makes one 8-inch tart shell.*

Grilled Chicken Tortas

W. PARK KERR / REPRINTED FROM *THE EL PASO CHILE COMPANY MARGARITA COOKBOOK*
(WILLIAM MORROW)

1 large boneless, skinless chicken breast
(about 3/4 pound)
3/4 cup Charred Tomato Salsa Borracho
(*recipe follows*)
Salt to taste

1/2 large avocado, pitted and peeled
1/3 cup refried beans
Two 6-inch crusty sandwich rolls or baguette
segments, split, excess crumb removed
1/2 cup shredded Monterey Jack cheese
Sliced pickled jalapeño chiles, optional

✱ Split the chicken breast into halves, pound out and trim. In a nonreactive dish, marinate the chicken in ⅔ cup of the salsa (reserve the rest) for 1 hour.

✱ Prepare a medium-hot fire in the grill.

✱ Lay the chicken breasts on the grill rack and spread with about half of the salsa from the dish. Cover and grill for 5 minutes. Turn, spread with the remaining salsa in the dish, and grill until just cooked through but still moist, another 4 to 5 minutes. Transfer to a cutting board and cool slightly, then thinly slice across the grain. Season lightly with salt.

✱ Meanwhile, in a bowl, mash the avocado. Stir in the reserved salsa and season with salt. Heat the beans (for a quantity this small, it's easiest to use the microwave oven).

✱ Spread the hot beans on the bottoms of the rolls. Sprinkle the beans with the cheese. Top the cheese with the chicken. Spread the avocado mixture over the chicken. Scatter the chile slices, if using, over the avocado. Close the sandwiches and serve.

Charred Tomato Salsa Borracho

3 large ripe tomatoes (1 1/2 pounds total)
1/3 cup minced white onion
4 cloves garlic, coarsely chopped
1/4 cup tequila
3 tablespoons lime juice

1 to 1 1/2 fresh jalapeño chiles, stemmed
and coarsely chopped
3/4 teaspoon salt, or to taste
1/3 cup minced fresh cilantro

✱ Position a rack about 6 inches from the broiler and preheat the broiler. (You can also do this on a grill.) In a shallow broiler-proof pan, char the tomatoes, turning them once, until well blackened and soft, about 20 minutes total. Cool. Core the tomatoes, but do not peel, and coarsely chop.

✱ In a food processor, combine the tomatoes, any of their juices, the onion, garlic, tequila, lime juice, jalapeño and salt. Process until fairly smooth. The salsa can be prepared to this point 1 day ahead and refrigerated. Stir in the cilantro just before serving. *Makes about 2 cups.*

Wrap Classico

MARY CORPENING BARBER AND SARA CORPENING WHITEFORD / REPRINTED FROM *WRAPS* (CHRONICLE)

One 15 1/2-ounce can black beans, drained	1/4 cup chopped fresh cilantro
1/2 cup chopped red bell pepper, seeds and ribs discarded	1/4 cup picante sauce
	1 tablespoon hot adobo marinade
1/2 cup chopped yellow bell pepper, seeds and ribs discarded	1/2 teaspoon ground cumin
	Two 10- or 11-inch flour tortillas
3/4 cup cooked long-grain white rice, warm	1/2 cup grated Monterey Jack cheese

✳ Heat the beans in a large saucepan over medium heat. Stir in the pepper, rice, cilantro, picante sauce, adobo marinade and cumin; cook until warm, 2 to 3 minutes.

✳ Divide the bean mixture among the tortillas, top with the cheese and fold in the sides of each tortilla. Fold up the bottom of each tortilla and continue to roll up into a cylinder, enclosing the filling. Cut the wraps in half on the diagonal and serve.

SERVES 2

THIS wrap IS A BURRITO, FILLED WITH savory BLACK BEANS, CRUNCHY PEPPERS, RICE AND MEXICAN seasonings, IT IS THE MOST CONVENTIONAL mixture. LOOK FOR ADOBO MARINADE IN A Latin MARKET, OR SUBSTITUTE A flavorful ENCHILADA SAUCE.

Hot Chili Pie

BILL HUFNAGLE/REPRINTED FROM *BIKER BILLY'S FREEWAY-A-FIRE* **(WILLIAM MORROW)**

1/4 cup olive oil
2 medium onions, diced
2 chipotle chiles packed in adobo sauce, minced
2 tablespoons chopped garlic
2 tablespoons Liquid Smoke
1/2 teaspoon ground cumin
1/2 teaspoon ground coriander
1 tablespoon dried parsley
1 tablespoon dried cilantro
1/2 teaspoon salt

1/2 teaspoon freshly ground black pepper
1/4 cup water
One 16-ounce can red kidney beans, drained and rinsed
One 16-ounce can cannellini beans, drained and rinsed
One 28-ounce can whole peeled tomatoes, coarsely chopped, with their juice
1 package pie crust mix (for a double-crust 9-inch pie)
3 cups shredded mild cheddar cheese

✳ Heat the olive oil in a large skillet over high heat. Add the onions and chipotle chiles and cook until the onions are golden brown, 6 to 8 minutes. Add the garlic and cook for 1 minute. Add the Liquid Smoke, cumin, coriander, parsley, cilantro, salt, pepper and water and stir well. Cook until the liquid is gone and the onions begin to fry again. Add the kidney and cannellini beans and stir well. Cook until the mixture begins to stick to the pan, 6 to 8 minutes. Add the tomatoes, stir well and bring to a boil. Reduce the heat to medium. Simmer, stirring often, until the sauce thickens, about 30 minutes. Remove from the heat and let cool to room temperature (if the filling is hot it will melt the pie crust during assembly). Add the cheese and stir until well blended.

✳ Preheat the oven to 450°F. Prepare the pie crust mix according to the package directions for two 9-inch pie crusts. Line two 9-inch pie pans with the crusts and flute the edges by pinching the dough between your thumb and forefinger. Divide the filling mixture between the two pie crusts and cover equally with the cheese. Bake until the cheese is melted and the crust is golden brown, 15 to 20 minutes. Serve warm, cut into wedges.

MAKES TWO 9-INCH PIES; SERVES 8 TO 12

THE golden, FLAKY PIE CRUST IS THE perfect COMPLEMENT TO THE FIERY FLAVORS OF THE FILLING. SMOKY CHIPOTLE FLAVOR, boosted BY LIQUID SMOKE, COMBINE WITH THE MEXICAN HERBS AND spices TO DELIVER A SOUTH-OF-THE-BORDER BLAST. THE AMPLE MEASURE OF CHEESE RICHLY ROUNDS OUT THE flavors. LOOK FOR CANNED chipotle CHILES IN A LATINO MARKET.

Homemade Cheese Blintzes

ALAN ROSEN/REPRINTED FROM *WELCOME TO JUNIOR'S!* (WILLIAM MORROW)

Crêpes
1 cup all-purpose flour
3 tablespoons sugar
1 tablespoon cornstarch
4 extra-large eggs
1 cup water
2 tablespoons unsalted butter, melted, plus
   2 to 3 tablespoons for cooking the
   crêpes and filled blintzes
1 tablespoon vegetable oil

Cheese Filling
1 pound cream cheese (do not substitute
   light)
1 cup large-curd cottage cheese (pot style)
$2/3$ cup sugar
1 teaspoon pure vanilla extract

Applesauce (optional)
Sour Cream (optional)
Fresh Strawberry Sauce (*recipe follows*,
   optional)

✳ Mix the flour, sugar and cornstarch together in a small bowl and set aside.

✳ With an electric mixer on high speed, beat the eggs, water, 2 tablespoons butter and oil together until light yellow in color. Reduce the speed to low and blend in the flour mixture all at once, just until the white disappears. (Do not overbeat at this stage, as this can cause the crêpes to be tough.)

✳ Preheat a 6-inch crêpe pan, or small skillet with sloping slides, over medium heat until a droplet of water sprinkled on the bottom of the pan sizzles. Brush the preheated pan with butter, coating it well.

✳ For each crêpe, pour about ¼ cup of the batter into the pan and immediately tilt the pan so the batter, completely but lightly, coats the bottom (don't worry if some of the batter moves up the sides of the pan about ¼ inch). Cook for about 30 seconds until the bottom of the crêpe is golden brown (just lift the edge to see).

✳ Loosen the crêpe by shaking the pan, then gently turn the crepe over with a spatula, being careful not to tear it. Cook the crêpe on the underside for only about 15 seconds, just until it's set. Turn the crêpes, light underside-up, onto a cooling rack. Refrigerate the crêpes, stacked slightly askew, for up to 2 days or freeze for up to 1 month.

✳ To make the cheese filling, stir all of the ingredients together in a small bowl until well blended.

✳ To fill each crêpe, spoon 3 tablespoons of filling in the center on the underside of the crêpe, then fold the edges over like an envelope.

✳ To fry the blintzes, melt 2 to 3 tablespoons butter in a large skillet over medium heat. Place the filled crêpes in the skillet, folded-ends down. Fry the blintzes until golden and hot on both sides, turning once, about 5 minutes total. Serve hot with applesauce, sour cream, or fresh strawberry sauce.

Fresh Strawberry Sauce

3 quarts fresh ripe strawberries	3 tablespoons cornstarch
1¼ cups cold water	Few drops red food coloring (optional)
1½ cups sugar	1 teaspoon vanilla extract

✳ Wash, sort through, hull and slice the strawberries ½-inch thick. Bring 1 cup of the water and the sugar to a boil in a medium saucepan over high heat. Boil for 5 minutes. Mix the cornstarch and the remaining ¼ cup water together in a cup until the cornstarch is thoroughly dissolved. Slowly whisk this mixture into the syrup. Return the mixture to a full boil and boil for 2 minutes.

✳ Remove the syrup from the heat and whisk in the food coloring, if using. Stir in the vanilla and gently fold in the strawberries. Store covered in the refrigerator for up to 3 days or in the freezer for up to 1 month. *Makes 1 quart.*

MAIN DISHES

Grilled Ginger Teriyaki Tuna

NINA SIMONDS/REPRINTED FROM *A SPOONFUL OF GINGER* (KNOPF)

2 pounds sushi-grade tuna

Ginger-Teriyaki Marinade
1/3 cup soy sauce
1/3 cup rice wine or sake
4 1/2 tablespoons sugar
1 1/2 tablespoons minced fresh ginger

1/2 teaspoon crushed red pepper flakes (optional)
1 1/2 tablespoons cornstarch
1/2 cup water

2 teaspoons canola or corn oil
3 tablespoons minced green onions

✳ Rinse the tuna under cold water and drain thoroughly in a colander. Cut the tuna into 6 pieces and place in a bowl.

✳ Mix the ginger teriyaki marinade ingredients in a medium saucepan and heat until thickened, stirring constantly over medium heat with a wooden spoon to prevent lumps. Remove the saucepan from the heat and let cool. Pour the marinade over the tuna and rub the mixture all over with your hands. Cover with plastic wrap and let the tuna marinate at room temperature for 1 hour, if possible.

✳ Prepare a medium-hot fire for grilling, and brush the grill lightly with the oil. Place the grill grate about 3 inches above the coals. Arrange the tuna on the grill and cook for about 3 to 4 minutes on each side for rare and 5 to 6 minutes for medium-rare.

✳ Alternatively, you can sear the fish in a heavy skillet, heating the pan until it is very hot, brushing it with oil and searing the tuna on both sides, covered, over very high heat.

✳ Distribute the tuna on plates, sprinkle the green onions on top and serve immediately.

SERVES 6

THE MULTIPURPOSE teriyaki SAUCE THAT GILDS THIS TUNA IS AN excellent MARINADE FOR ANY GRILLED OR PAN-SEARED SEAFOOD. Sushi-grade TUNA REFERS TO THE HIGHEST QUALITY AND choicest CUTS OF THE FISH THAT ARE AVAILABLE ON THE MARKET. IT IS IMPORTANT TO LOOK FOR THIS GRADE OF tuna WHEN PREPARING FISH THAT WILL NOT BE COOKED ALL THE WAY THROUGH.

Grilled Scallops with Rainbow Peppers, Wilted Greens and Fresh Cilantro Dressing

NINA SIMONDS/REPRINTED FROM *A SPOONFUL OF GINGER* (KNOPF)

SERVES 6

YOU CAN PREPARE
THIS favorite SUMMER
LUNCH OR LIGHT DINNER
ENTRÉE IN advance.
DEPENDING ON AVAILABILITY,
YOU CAN substitute
SHRIMP OR SQUID FOR
THE SCALLOPS.

Ginger Marinade
2 tablespoons rice wine or sake
2 tablespoons soy sauce
1 tablespoon minced fresh ginger
1 teaspoon toasted sesame oil

1 red bell pepper, cored, seeded and cut into 1^1/$_2$-inch squares
1 yellow bell pepper, cored, seeded and cut into 1^1/$_2$-inch squares
1 orange bell pepper, cored, seeded and cut into 1^1/$_2$-inch squares
1^1/$_2$ pounds sea scallops, rinsed and drained, side muscle removed
Six to eight 10-inch bamboo or metal skewers (if bamboo, soaked in cold water to cover for 1 hour)

Fresh Cilantro Dressing
^{1}/$_3$ cup soy sauce
^{1}/$_4$ cup clear rice vinegar
2 tablespoons toasted sesame oil
1^1/$_2$ tablespoons sugar
1^1/$_2$ tablespoons rice wine or sake
^{1}/$_3$ cup chopped fresh cilantro leaves

1 pound snow pea shoots, tender spinach or other baby greens, rinsed and drained
2 teaspoons canola or corn oil
2 teaspoons minced garlic
2 tablespoons rice wine or sake
1 teaspoon salt

✳ Mix the ginger marinade ingredients in a bowl. Thread the peppers and the scallops onto the skewers, starting and ending with the peppers. Brush the scallops and peppers with the marinade and let stand, covered, for at least 30 minutes.

✳ Mix the cilantro dressing ingredients in another bowl. Trim any wilted or hard stems from the snow pea shoots or baby greens and place near the stove. Pour the cilantro dressing into a serving container.

✳ Heat a wok or large skillet, add the oil and heat until near smoking. Add the greens and garlic and toss lightly for about 20 seconds. Add the rice wine and salt and toss lightly over high heat for about 1 minute or less, until the greens are slightly wilted but still bright green. Spoon the greens onto a serving platter and mound slightly so that the scallops can be arranged on top.

✳ Prepare a fire for grilling and arrange the skewers of scallops and peppers about 3 inches from the heat source. Broil or grill for about 3 to 4 minutes on each side, turning once and brushing with the marinade. Arrange the cooked scallops and peppers over the wilted greens, leaving them on the skewers or removing them. Spoon the cilantro dressing on top or serve on the side. Serve warm.

Corn-Wrapped Salmon and Scallops

JAMES MCNAIR/REPRINTED FROM *JAMES MCNAIR'S FAVORITES* **(CHRONICLE)**

SERVES 4

THE summer

COMBINATION OF GRILLED

SALMON AND garden-

fresh CORN IS AN UNBEAT-

ABLE ONE. HERE'S AN

UNUSUAL PRESENTATION OF

THE classic PAIRING.

ALTHOUGH CERTAINLY NOT

PICTURESQUE, ALUMINUM

FOIL CAN BE USED INSTEAD

OF THE CORN husks.

4 ears corn, unshucked
One 1-pound salmon fillet, skinned and
　　cut into 4 equal pieces
1 pound small sea scallops, or 1 pound
　　larger scallops, cut into small pieces
¼ cup freshly squeezed lemon juice

4 green onions, including the green tops,
　　thinly sliced
Salt and freshly ground black pepper
　　to taste
¼ cup (½ stick) unsalted butter
Vegetable oil for brushing grill grate

✳ Prepare a hot fire in the grill.

✳ Remove the husks and silks from the corn, being careful not to tear the husks and keeping them as fully intact as possible. Remove 1 sturdy leaf from each set of husks and cut each of these lengthwise into 2 strips; reserve all of the husks.

✳ Rest the base of an ear of shucked corn in a large, deep plate or inside a large bowl. With a sharp knife, cut down the length of the cob from the tip to the base. Leave behind a bit of the pulp to avoid mixing tough cob fibers into the corn kernels. Turn the knife blade over and scrape the cob with the blunt edge to remove the pulp and milky juices; set aside.

✳ Quickly rinse the salmon and scallops under cold running water, pat dry with paper towels and set aside.

✳ Spread out the 4 sets of corn husks on a flat surface, making sure the leaves overlap to prevent leakage during cooking. Spoon ¼ of the corn kernels into the center of each husk set. Top the corn with a piece of salmon and ¼ of the scallops. Sprinkle each packet with lemon juice, green onions, salt and pepper, and dot with the butter. Bring the husks together to enclose the contents completely and tie each end with a strip of husk.

✳ When the fire is ready, lightly brush the grill grate with oil. Place the packets on the grate and grill, turning once, until the salmon is just opaque when cut into at the thickest part with a small sharp knife, about 10 minutes (test by opening a packet, then retie the packet for serving).

✳ Transfer the packets to warmed plates and serve immediately, allowing the diners to open the packets at the table.

Steamed Lemon Chicken

EILEEN YIN-FEI LO/REPRINTED FROM *THE CHINESE KITCHEN* **(WILLIAM MORROW)**

1 chicken (about 4 pounds)
4 tablespoons salt
1 1/4 lemons, whole lemon cut into quarters

Marinade
1 tablespoon Chinese rice wine or gin
1 teaspoon ginger juice
1 1/2 tablespoons light soy sauce
1 1/2 tablespoons oyster sauce

2 teaspoons sesame oil
1 tablespoon peanut oil
2 teaspoons salt
2 teaspoons sugar
1/8 teaspoon freshly ground white pepper
3 1/2 tablespoons cornstarch

2 tablespoons finely sliced green onions
Hot cooked rice for accompaniment

✴ Rinse the chicken and remove the fat and extra membranes. Rub the chicken with 2 tablespoons of the salt and rinse again under cold running water. Thoroughly pat the chicken dry with paper towels. Place the chicken in a bowl. Squeeze the lemon quarters over the chicken and place the quarters in the bowl. Add the marinade ingredients to the bowl and mix well. Let the mixture stand for 30 minutes.

✴ Place the chicken on a heatproof dish and spread it out on the plate. Pour the marinade evenly over the chicken. Place the dish in a bamboo steamer, cover the steamer and place it over simmering water. Steam the chicken for 40 to 50 minutes, turning it 2 to 3 times during steaming. The chicken is done when it turns white.

✴ Turn off the heat and remove the top of the steamer. Present the chicken in the dish, in the steamer, sprinkled with the green onions. Accompany servings with the rice.

SERVES 6 TO 8

IN MOST RECIPES FOR CHINESE lemon CHICKEN, THE MEAT IS COATED AND FRIED, AND SERVED WITH A CORNSTARCH-THICKENED sauce. IN THIS RECIPE, FROM EILEEN'S family, THE CHICKEN IS STEAMED WITH fresh LEMON QUARTERS—A REFRESHING ALTERNATIVE.

MAKE YOUR OWN FRESH ginger JUICE IN A JUICE EXTRACTOR OR LOOK FOR IT AT THE LOCAL juice BAR.

Apple Cider-Poached Chicken with Black Currant Barley

JIM COLEMAN/REPRINTED FROM *THE RITTENHOUSE COOKBOOK* (TEN SPEED)

1 red apple, preferably Macintosh or Jonathan, peeled, cored and diced
5 cups fresh apple cider
1 cinnamon stick, coarsely broken
5 whole cloves
2 whole allspice berries
4 boneless, skinless chicken breasts, about 6 ounces each
1/2 tablespoon olive oil

1 tablespoon minced garlic
2 tablespoons minced shallots
1 cup uncooked barley
2 1/2 cups low-sodium chicken broth
3/4 cup dried black currants
1 tablespoon minced fresh basil
1/2 tablespoon minced fresh oregano
2 tablespoons diced red apple, preferably Macintosh or Jonathan, for garnish

✳ Combine the apple, cider, cinnamon, cloves and allspice in a large saucepan and bring to a boil. Reduce the heat and simmer for 8 to 10 minutes. Reduce the heat to just under a simmer (low enough to stop the broth from simmering but still keeping it hot). Add the chicken breasts and poach for about 15 minutes, or until cooked through. Remove the chicken from the broth and cover with aluminum foil to keep warm.

✳ Heat the olive oil in a saucepan and sauté the garlic and shallots over medium-high heat for 2 minutes, or until the shallots are translucent. Stir in the barley, add the broth, and simmer over medium-low heat for 20 minutes. Add the currants and continue simmering for 10 minutes longer, or until all of the liquid has evaporated. Remove from the heat and stir in the basil and oregano.

✳ Spoon a bed of the barley mixture on each serving plate and place a chicken breast on top. Garnish the chicken with the diced apples.

Smothered Chicken

JOYCE WHITE/REPRINTED FROM *SOUL FOOD* (HARPERCOLLINS)

1 chicken (about 3 to 3 1/2 pounds)	2 onions
1 teaspoon salt	2 cloves garlic
1/2 teaspoon freshly ground black pepper	1/2 teaspoon dried thyme
1/2 cup flour	2 tablespoons oil
1 celery stalk	2 cups chicken broth

✱ Cut the chicken into serving pieces: the breast into halves, the legs and thighs separated, plus the wings, for a total of 8 pieces. Trim away any visible fat and discard. Rinse the chicken well under cold running water. Pat dry with paper towels.

✱ Sprinkle the chicken with the salt and black pepper. Place the chicken in a plastic or brown bag. Pour the flour into the bag and shake well to cover the chicken all over. Remove the chicken from the bag and dust off the excess flour. Save 1 tablespoon of the flour to use to thicken the gravy.

✱ Dice the celery, slice the onions, and mince the garlic. Crush the thyme.

✱ Heat the oil in a large skillet that has a cover. Add the chicken and sauté over medium-low heat for about 20 minutes, turning occasionally to brown evenly. When golden brown, push the chicken to the side of the pan. Add the reserved tablespoon of flour and sauté, stirring, until lightly browned.

✱ Add the celery, onion and garlic to the skillet and sauté for 5 minutes, stirring occasionally, or until the vegetables are tender. Stir together the chicken and vegetables.

✱ Add the thyme and chicken broth. Bring to a gentle boil. Reduce the heat to very low, cover, and simmer the chicken for 20 to 25 minutes, or until the chicken is fork-tender and the juices run clear when pierced. Serve hot.

SERVES 4

FOR THIS southern-style MAIN DISH, A CUT-UP CHICKEN IS "smothered" WITH SAVORY VEGETABLES AND CHICKEN BROTH. IT'S A perfect HOME-STYLE MEAL FOR A COOL FALL EVENING.

SERVES 4 TO 6

SINCE THE CHICKEN AND VEGETABLES marinate overnight, YOU MUST START THIS dish THE DAY BEFORE YOU PLAN TO eat IT.

Easy Kid Kabobs

REPRINTED FROM *THE HOLE IN THE WALL GANG COOKBOOK* **(SIMON AND SCHUSTER)**

1 pint (2 cups) cherry tomatoes
1 red onion
1 green bell pepper
1 pint (2 cups) mushrooms

2 whole boneless, skinless chicken breasts, cut into "nuggets"
One 16-ounce bottle Newman's Own Light Italian dressing, or your favorite

✱ Wash and dice the tomatoes, onion, pepper and mushrooms.

✱ Place the diced vegetables and chicken in a medium bowl. Pour the Italian dressing over them and mix well. Cover and refrigerate overnight.

✱ When ready to serve, preheat the oven to 350°F.

✱ Arrange the chicken and vegetables on skewers. Place in a baking dish and bake for 30 to 40 minutes, rotating the skewers after 15 to 20 minutes. Serve warm.

SPECIAL NOTE: Debbie Fullerton's class at Cesar Chavez School in Indio, California, won a prize with this healthy recipe for chicken and vegetable kabobs, marinated in Newman's Own Light Italian Dressing to add zip and zest. The fourth graders donated their charity award to the Children's Museum of the Desert.

Butterflied Chicken Under Bricks

JAMIE PURVIANCE/REPRINTED FROM *WEBER'S ART OF THE GRILL* **(CHRONICLE)**

1/4 cup orange juice concentrate (undiluted)
1/4 cup mild chili sauce
2 tablespoons dark molasses
1 tablespoon soy sauce
2 teaspoons whole-grain mustard
1 tablespoon white wine vinegar
1 teaspoon Worcestershire sauce
1/2 teaspoon Tabasco sauce

1/2 teaspoon kosher salt
2 chickens (about 3 pounds each)
Kosher salt and freshly ground black
    pepper to taste
Vegetable oil for brushing grill grate
Nonstick cooking spray for greasing
    baking sheet
3 bricks, wrapped in aluminum foil

✳ Preheat the grill to high.

✳ In a small saucepan, combine the orange juice concentrate, chili sauce, molasses, soy sauce, mustard, white wine vinegar, Worcestershire sauce, Tabasco sauce and 1/2 teaspoon salt. Bring to a boil, then simmer for about 5 minutes. Remove from the heat and let cool to room temperature.

✳ Place one chicken on a cutting board, breast-side up. Position a heavy knife or poultry shears inside the cavity, and cut through the ribs along one side of the backbone. Make a second cut through the ribs along the other side of the backbone. Remove any bones that stick up. Repeat with the second chicken. Season both sides of the chickens with salt and pepper.

✳ Lightly brush the grill grate with vegetable oil. Place the chickens, skin-side down, over indirect high heat. Lightly coat the bottom of a baking sheet with cooking spray. Place the baking sheet on top of the chickens and weight them down with the bricks. Grill the chickens indirectly over high heat for 30 minutes. Using thick pot holders, remove the bricks and the baking sheet. If the skin is crispy and the juices run clear, the chickens are ready to serve. If not, continue to grill them indirectly over high heat, but without the baking sheet and bricks. Remove the chickens when the meat is opaque throughout and the juices run clear.

✳ Cut the chickens into quarters. Serve warm with the barbecue sauce.

SERVES 4 TO 6

FLATTENING A CHICKEN UNDER THE WEIGHT OF A brick MAY SEEM GIMMICKY, BUT THE TECHNIQUE helps THE MEAT TO COOK MORE EVENLY AND PROMOTES A crispier SKIN. THE ACCOMPANYING BARBECUE SAUCE, WHICH tastes SWEET AND tangy AT FIRST, THEN BUILDS SLOWLY IN heat, HAS AUTHENTIC KANSAS CITY CHARACTER.

Piri-Piri Chicken

STEVEN RAICHLEN/REPRINTED FROM *THE BARBECUE BIBLE* **(WORKMAN)**

SERVES 4 TO 8

PIRI-PIRI IS THE PORTUGUESE NAME FOR A hot sauce MADE WITH TINY fiery chiles AND VINEGAR. NOTE THAT AT BRAZILIAN markets, PIRI-PIRI GOES BY THE NAME OF *MOLHO MALAGUETA* (MALAGUETA PEPPER SAUCE).

2 whole chickens (about 3 1/2 to 4 pounds each)
1/2 cup extra-virgin olive oil
8 tablespoons (1 stick) salted butter, melted
1/3 cup fresh lemon juice
3 to 4 tablespoons malagueta pepper sauce, or other hot pepper sauce
1 tablespoon sweet paprika
1 teaspoon ground coriander
3 cloves garlic
3 green onions, sliced
3 tablespoons coarsely chopped Italian parsley
One 1-inch piece fresh ginger, thinly sliced
2 bay leaves, crumbled
1/2 teaspoon salt
1/2 teaspoon freshly ground black pepper
Vegetable oil for brushing grill grate

✳ Remove and discard the fat just inside the body cavities of the chickens. Remove the packages of giblets and set aside for another use. Rinse the chickens, inside and out, under cold running water, then drain and blot dry, inside and out, with paper towels.

✳ Place the birds, breast-sides down, on a cutting board. Using poultry shears, cut through the flesh and bone along both sides of the backbones. Cut from the tail ends to the head ends and completely remove the backbones. Open out the birds, like opening a book, by gently pulling the halves apart. Using a sharp paring knife, lightly score the top of the breastbones. Run your thumbs along and under the sides of the breastbones and attached cartilage and pop them out. Spread the birds out flat. Turn the birds over.

✳ Using a sharp knife, make a slit in the skin between the lower end of the breastbones and the legs, on each side, 1 inch long. Stick the ends of the drumsticks through the slits (this step is optional, but it gives you a more attractive bird). Place the chickens in a large nonreactive bowl or baking dish and set aside while you prepare the marinade/sauce.

✳ Combine the oil, melted butter, lemon juice, hot sauce, paprika, coriander, garlic, green onions, parsley, ginger, bay leaves, salt and pepper in a blender and process to a smooth puree. Pour 1/2 of this sauce over the chickens in the bowl and coat the chickens with it, using your hands. Set aside the remaining mixture to serve with the chickens. Cover and let the chickens marinate, in the refrigerator, for 4 to 12 hours (the longer the better); transfer the remaining sauce to a small bowl and refrigerate, covered, until serving time. Bring the sauce to room temperature before serving.

✳ Set up the grill for indirect grilling, placing one large or two smaller drip pans in the center, and preheat to medium.

✳ When ready to cook, oil the grill grate. Place the chickens, skin-side up, on the hot grate, reserving any marinade in the bowl. Brush the chickens with the marinade, then cover the grill and cook for 30 minutes. Uncover and brush the chickens with any remaining marinade. Cover again and continue grilling the chickens until the juices run clear when the tip of a skewer or sharp knife is inserted in the thickest part of a thigh, or an instant-read thermometer inserted in the inner muscle of a thigh registers 180°F, 30 to 40 minutes more. If a crisp skin is desired, place the chickens, skin-side down, on the grill grate directly over the fire for the last 5 to 10 minutes.

✳ Using long spatulas, carefully transfer the chickens to a cutting board or platter and let stand for 5 minutes before carving. Serve accompanied by the reserved sauce.

NOTE: For a smokier flavor, you can cook the chickens using the direct method rather than the indirect method. Preheat the grill to medium, oil the grate, and add the chickens to the hot grate skin-side down. Grill, uncovered, for 15 to 20 minutes per side, turning the birds very carefully with long spatulas so they stay in one piece.

Roast Breast of Turkey with Cornbread, Spinach and Pecans

MARLENE SOROSKY/REPRINTED FROM *ENTERTAINING ON THE RUN* (WILLIAM MORROW)

1 whole turkey breast, skinned, boned and butterflied (about 5^1/$_2$ to 7 pounds with bones, 4 to 5 pounds without bones)

Marinade
Juice and grated zest of 3 medium oranges (about 1 cup juice)
^{2}/$_3$ cup balsamic vinegar
^{1}/$_4$ cup olive oil
^{1}/$_4$ cup honey

Stuffing
1 tablespoon olive oil
2 onions, chopped
2 cups chopped fresh spinach (bite-sized pieces)
1^1/$_2$ cups packaged cornbread stuffing, such as Pepperidge Farm

2^1/$_2$ cups coarsely chopped pecans, toasted
1 tablespoon prepared mustard
^{1}/$_4$ cup chicken broth
2 large eggs, lightly beaten

Salt and freshly ground black pepper to taste
1 cup dry red wine, plus more to taste
^{1}/$_4$ cup chicken broth
^{1}/$_4$ cup honey, plus more to taste
1 egg white, mixed with 1 teaspoon water
1 tablespoon cornstarch, mixed with 1 tablespoon water

Greens, such as spinach or parsley, for garnish (optional)
Orange slices, for garnish (optional)

✳ Rinse and dry the turkey breast. Pound the turkey lightly to make it as even as possible and place it in a shallow nonaluminum dish.

✳ To make the marinade, mix the juice, zest, vinegar, oil, and honey in a small bowl. Pour over the turkey, turning to coat both sides. Cover and refrigerate overnight, turning once or twice.

✳ To make the stuffing, heat the oil in a large skillet over medium heat. Add the onions and sauté until tender, about 10 minutes. Stir in the spinach and sauté until wilted. Transfer to a large bowl and stir in the cornbread stuffing, pecans, mustard, broth and eggs.

✳ Preheat the oven to 375°F. Remove the turkey from the marinade. Dry it well and place it on a work surface, skin-side down. Pour the marinade into a deep saucepan and set aside. Sprinkle the meat with salt and pepper and spread with ½ of the stuffing. Beginning with a short end, roll the meat up like a jelly roll; do not be concerned about torn or uneven pieces of meat. Tie the meat with kitchen string at 1-inch intervals. Sprinkle with salt and pepper.

✷ Place the turkey in a shallow roasting pan, add about ½ inch of water and roast for 50 to 60 minutes, or until a meat thermometer reaches 120°F. Baste with the pan drippings every 15 minutes and add more water to the pan as needed.

✷ While the turkey roasts, pour the wine and broth into the saucepan with the marinade to make a sauce. Simmer over medium heat until reduced by about half. Set aside.

✷ Transfer the turkey to a cutting board. Pour the drippings into the sauce. Stir 1 tablespoon of the sauce into the honey. Cut the strings off of the turkey, brush the top and sides with egg white and press the remaining stuffing firmly over the top and sides. Drizzle with ½ of the honey mixture. Return to the oven and roast for 15 minutes. Drizzle with the remaining honey mixture and roast for 15 more minutes, or until the exterior is brown and crusty and a thermometer inserted into the center reaches 145° to 150°F. Transfer the roast to a cutting board and let it rest for 20 minutes before carving. (The turkey can be cooled to room temperature, wrapped in foil and refrigerated overnight. To reheat, bring it to room temperature, return to the roasting pan, add ½ inch broth or water, cover loosely with foil and roast at 375°F for 30 minutes, or until heated through.)

✷ To complete the sauce, deglaze the roasting pan by placing it on the stovetop over medium-high heat. Add a little of the sauce and bring to a boil, scraping the bottom of the pan and stirring constantly. Strain into the remaining sauce in the saucepan. Remove from the heat and whisk in the cornstarch. Return to the heat and cook, whisking, until the sauce comes to a boil and thickens. Season to taste with salt and pepper, and more wine and/or honey, if needed. (The sauce can be refrigerated overnight. Reheat until bubbling before serving.)

✷ To serve, carve the roast into ⅛-inch slices, arrange overlapping on a platter, drizzle with the sauce, and, if desired, garnish with greens and oranges.

SERVES 3 TO 4

TURKEY IS EXTREMELY popular IN PARISIAN HOMES, BUT SINCE IT'S NOT A traditional HOLIDAY FEAST, YOU RARELY EVER SEE A WHOLE BIRD FOR SALE. OFTEN PARISIANS BUY BONELESS BREASTS THAT THE butcher HAS SEASONED AND TIED INTO ROASTS. THIS TURKEY BREAST absorbs THE FLAVOR OF THE CARAMEL-IZED ONIONS WITH WHICH IT'S COOKED, AND BECOMES lusciously SWEET.

Pan-Roasted Turkey Breast with Onion Marmalade

MICHAEL ROBERTS/REPRINTED FROM *PARISIAN HOME COOKING* (WILLIAM MORROW)

4 small sprigs fresh rosemary
1 boneless turkey breast (about 1 1/2 to 2 pounds)
Salt and freshly ground black pepper
4 tablespoons (1/2 stick) unsalted butter
5 medium onions, finely chopped (about 2 1/2 cups)
1/8 teaspoon freshly grated nutmeg
1 cup dry white wine, such as Chardonnay
1 cup low-sodium chicken broth

✱ Insert the sprigs of rosemary under the skin of the turkey, then lay it skin-side down and season with salt and pepper. Tie the breast with butcher's twine to form a compact cylinder and season the skin with salt and pepper.

✱ Melt 2 tablespoons of the butter in a large skillet over medium heat. Add the turkey and cook until light golden brown on all sides, 8 to 10 minutes. Transfer the turkey to a plate and set aside.

✱ Reduce the heat to medium-low, add the onions, nutmeg and salt to taste, and cook, stirring occasionally, until the onions dry out and darken, 30 to 35 minutes.

✱ Place the turkey on top of the onions and pour in the wine and broth. Cover and cook until the turkey is tender, about 30 minutes. Transfer the turkey to a cutting board.

✱ Increase the heat to medium and cook until the cooking liquid reduces and thickens, about 5 minutes. Turn off the heat and swirl in the remaining 2 tablespoons butter.

✱ Untie the turkey and slice it into serving pieces. Pour any collected juices into the onions. Scrape the onions onto a platter, arrange the sliced turkey on top and serve immediately.

Grilled Pork Tenderloin
with Rosemary and Fennel Seed Crust

BRUCE AIDELLS/REPRINTED FROM *THE COMPLETE MEAT COOKBOOK* **(HOUGHTON MIFFILIN)**

2 pork tenderloins, (about ³/₄ to 1¹/₄ pounds each) trimmed of silverskin and fat

1 tablespoon olive oil

1 tablespoon fennel seeds, bruised with the flat side of a knife or with a mortar and pestle

1 tablespoon chopped fresh rosemary, or 2 teaspoons dried

1 tablespoon minced garlic

2 teaspoons kosher salt

2 teaspoons coarsely ground black pepper

✱ Butterfy the pork by cutting lengthwise down the center. Pound the tenderloins to a ⅛- to ½-inch thickness.

✱ Spread the meat on a plate and rub the olive oil on both sides. Combine the remaining ingredients in a bowl and rub the mixture all over the pork, pressing it into the meat and any crevices. Let the tenderloins stand for 30 minutes at room temperature.

✱ Grill the tenderloins over medium-hot coals for 3 to 4 minutes per side, or until the internal temperature registers 145° to 150°F on an instant-read thermometer. Let the tenderloins stand, covered lightly with for 10 minutes. Serve one half tenderloin per person; serve warm.

SERVES 4 TO 6

THE savory HERB CRUST THAT COATS THIS TENDERLOIN CAN ALSO BE USED TO coat PORK, LAMB OR VEAL CHOPS. Roasted OR GRILLED FENNEL BULBS, OR BRAISED RED OR GREEN CABBAGE, WOULD BE A nice COMPLEMENT.

SERVES 4

SICILIAN IN style, THIS DISH FEATURES A SAUCE— actually MORE LIKE A jam—OF TOMATOES, VINEGAR AND SUGAR. BE SURE TO FULLY COMPLETE EACH REDUCTION WITH THE vinegar AND TOMATOES IN ORDER TO achieve THE CORRECT FLAVOR.

Garlic-Caper Grilled Pork Chops

LYNNE ROSSETTO KASPER/REPRINTED FROM *THE ITALIAN COUNTRY TABLE* (SCRIBNER)

3 tablespoons salted capers, soaked for 10 minutes in cold water and drained, or 3 tablespoons capers in vinegar, drained
3 large cloves garlic
1 tightly packed tablespoon fresh rosemary leaves

1 tablespoon fruity extra-virgin olive oil
1/8 to 1/4 teaspoon freshly ground black pepper
Four 1-inch-thick rib or loin pork chops (if possible, hormone- and antibiotic-free)
Salt to taste
Sicilian Sauce (*recipe follows*)

✳ One day before cooking, mince together, in a food processor or by hand, the capers, garlic and rosemary. Blend in the oil and pepper. Coat both sides of the chops with the caper mixture, set on a plate, cover and refrigerate overnight.

✳ The next day, grill the chops on a medium-hot hard-wood charcoal fire (white ashes covering the charcoal), or grill indoors using a griddled skillet or a 12-inch regular skillet, lightly filmed with oil, set over medium-high heat. Sprinkle the chops with salt and quickly brown them on both sides (don't worry if the seasonings fall away on the grill), then push the chops away from the hottest part of the grill, or lower the burner heat to medium-low. Cook for about 4 minutes per side, or until the chops are barely firm when pressed and lightly blushed with pink inside (150°F on an instant-read thermometer).

✳ Serve the chops hot, with a large spoonful of the Sicilian sauce on the side.

Sicilian Sauce

1 tablespoon extra-virgin olive oil
1/2 medium onion, minced
One 11/2-inch sprig rosemary
Salt and freshly ground black pepper
   to taste
3 tablespoons sugar
1/8 teaspoon dried oregano

1/4 teaspoon dried basil
Grated zest of 1 large orange
1 large clove garlic, minced
1/2 cup red wine vinegar
1 generous cup drained canned whole
   tomatoes

✴ In a 10-inch skillet, heat the oil over medium-high heat. Add the onion, rosemary and a generous sprinkling of salt and pepper. Sauté until the onion begins to color, then add the sugar. Stir with a wooden spatula as the sugar melts and bubbles (taking care not to burn), then finally turns pale amber, while the onions remain light colored.

✴ Immediately add the herbs, zest and garlic. Standing back to avoid splatters, quickly add the vinegar. Stir and boil down until the vinegar is a glaze, coating the onion and barely covering the bottom of the pan. Continue to scrape down the pan's sides, to bring the developing glaze back into the sauce; watch for burning.

✴ Stir in the tomatoes, crushing them with your hands as they go into the pan. Boil, scraping down the sides and stirring, until the sauce is almost sizzling in its own juices. It should be like a thick jam that mounds on a spoon. Finish seasoning with a few grinds of black pepper, turn out of the pan and cool. Serve at room temperature or warm. Store covered in the refrigerator. *Makes about 1 cup.*

Baby Back Pork Ribs
with Spicy Peanut Butter Slather

HUGH CARPENTER/REPRINTED FROM *GREAT RIBS* (TEN SPEED PRESS)

SERVES 4

BE generous WITH

THIS THICK, ASIAN-INSPIRED

marinade THAT COATS

BABY BACK RIBS. A good

LONG SOAK IN THE PEANUT

BUTTER-BASED BATH WILL

RENDER THESE tender

PORK RIBS IRRESISTIBLE.

2 sides pork baby back ribs, or your favorite ribs
1/2 cup chunky peanut butter
1/2 cup dry sherry or Chinese rice wine
1/4 cup soy sauce
1/4 cup honey
2 tablespoons dark sesame oil

2 tablespoons Asian chili sauce
Grated zest of 1 lime
6 cloves garlic, finely minced
1/4 cup finely minced fresh ginger
1/4 cup minced green onion
1/4 cup minced fresh cilantro

✳ Remove the membrane on the underside of the ribs and place the ribs in a rectangular dish. Combine the remaining ingredients in a bowl and stir well. Rub the marinade over the ribs, coating them evenly. Refrigerate. Marinate for at least 15 minutes. For more intense flavor, marinate for 8 hours.

✳ If using a gas grill, preheat it to medium (325°F). If using a charcoal or wood grill, prepare a fire. When the coals are ash covered, place a rib rack on the cooking grate and fit the ribs into the rack. Cover and grill until the meat shrinks away from the ends of the bones, about 1 hour. Occasionally during cooking, baste the ribs with extra marinade. Or, roast the ribs in a 325°F oven, placed on a wire rack, meaty side up. Do not turn the ribs over during the roasting process.

✳ To serve, cut each side of ribs in half, or into 3 sections, or into individual ribs. Transfer to a heated serving platter or heated dinner plates and serve at once.

Pork Loin with Apples, Cider and Calvados

COLMAN ANDREWS/REPRINTED FROM *SAVEUR COOKS AUTHENTIC FRENCH* (CHRONICLE)

SERVES 8 TO 10

Apples ARE A PRODUCT
OF THE NORMANDY REGION
OF NORTHERN France.
HERE THEY ARE USED IN
THREE FORMS TO accent
ROASTED PORK. CALVADOS,
A PRODUCT OF THE REGION,
IS brandy MADE FROM
INDIGENIUOS APPLES.

1 pork loin roast (about 4 1/2 pounds)
1 tablespoon flour
Salt and freshly ground black pepper
    to taste
2 teaspoons finely chopped fresh rosemary
1/4 cup (1/2 stick) butter
3 medium-sized yellow onions, chopped

2 cloves garlic, chopped
4 sprigs fresh rosemary (optional)
5 baking apples, cored and quartered
1/2 cup Sydre Argelette or other good-
    quality French hard cider
1/4 cup good-quality Calvados

✷ Preheat the oven to 325°F.

✷ Tie the pork at 2-inch intervals with kitchen string so that it holds a cylindrical shape. Mix together the flour, salt, pepper and chopped rosemary in a small bowl. Rub the flour mixture all over the pork loin, coating evenly and well.

✷ Heat 2 tablespoons of the butter in a large heavy skillet and sear the meat in the butter over high heat, turning often, until it is browned on all sides, about 15 minutes. Transfer the meat with pan juices to a large baking pan and scatter the onions and garlic around it. Cut up the remaining 2 tablespoons butter and distribute it evenly over the onions. Add the rosemary sprigs, if using, to the pan and cover the pan with foil.

✷ Place the pan in the oven and cook for 45 minutes, then add the apples and hard cider. Baste the pork and apples with the pan juices. Re-cover the pan and cook for another 30 minutes. Increase the oven heat to 400°F, remove the foil from the pan, baste the pork and apples with the pan juices and roast uncovered for 15 minutes.

✷ Transfer the roast to a cutting board, remove the string and allow it to stand for 10 minutes before slicing. Meanwhile, transfer the onions and apples to a platter. Place the pan on the stovetop over medium-high heat and cook until the pan juices are reduced by half, about 5 minutes.

✷ Warm the Calvados in a small pan, add it to the pan juices and carefully ignite the mixture with a long kitchen match (keep the pan lid nearby to extinguish the flames if necessary). Simmer the sauce while you slice the pork loin. Arrange the meat over the apples and onions and serve with the sauce.

Pepper Steak

EILEEN YIN-FEI LO / REPRINTED FROM *THE CHINESE KITCHEN* (WILLIAM MORROW)

SERVES 6

3/4 pound lean beef, preferably London Broil, cut across the grain into 1/4-inch slices, then into 2-inch pieces

Marinade

2 teaspoons oyster sauce
1 teaspoon sesame oil
1/2 teaspoon minced fresh ginger
1 1/2 teaspoons Shao-Hsing wine or sherry
3/4 teaspoon dark soy sauce
1/2 teaspoon salt
1 teaspoon sugar
1 1/2 teaspoons cornstarch
Pinch of white pepper

Sauce

2 teaspoons oyster sauce
1 teaspoon sesame oil
1 teaspoon dark soy sauce
1 teaspoon sugar
2 teaspoons cornstarch
Pinch of white pepper
1/2 cup chicken broth

2 large cloves garlic, smashed, skin removed
1 tablespoon fermented black beans, rinsed well and drained
3 tablespoons peanut oil
One 1/2-inch slice fresh ginger, peeled
1 medium-sized green bell pepper, cut into 2-by-1-inch pieces
1 medium-sized red bell pepper, cut into 2-by-1-inch pieces
Hot cooked rice for accompaniment

THIS recipe, WHICH COMES FROM EILEEN'S father, UTILIZES MANY ASIAN INGREDIENTS THAT MAY NOT BE FAMILIAR TO YOU. LOOK FOR SUCH INGREDIENTS AS Shao-Hsing WINE, DARK SOY SAUCE, OYSTER SAUCE AND FERMENTED BLACK BEANS IN AN Asian MARKET. YOU MAY ALSO FIND MANY OF THESE ITEMS IN YOUR NEIGHBORHOOD GROCERY store, IF IT HAS A WELL-STOCKED ASIAN SECTION.

✷ Place the beef in a bowl with the marinade ingredients and mix well. Let the mixture stand for 30 minutes. In another bowl, mix the sauce ingredients and set aside.

✷ Place the smashed garlic and black beans in a bowl and mash to a paste with the handle of a cleaver. Or, mash the ingredients with a mortar and pestle.

✷ Heat a wok over high heat for 30 seconds. Add 1 tablespoon of the peanut oil and spread out with a spatula. When a wisp of white smoke appears, add the ginger and stir-fry until the ginger turns light brown. Add the peppers and stir-fry for 1 minute. Turn off the heat and transfer the peppers to a small bowl. Wipe out the wok and spatula with paper towels.

✷ Heat the wok over high heat for 30 seconds. Add the remaining peanut oil and spread out with a spatula. When a wisp of white smoke appears, add the garlic-black bean paste and stir-fry until the garlic turns light brown. Add the beef and the marinade and spread out in a thin layer. Cook the beef, without stirring, for 1 minute, tipping the wok from side to side to ensure even cooking. Turn the beef over and cook for about 30 seconds. Add the peppers and stir-fry for 2 minutes.

✷ Make a well in the center of the beef-pepper mixture. Stir the sauce and pour it into the well. Stir-fry until the sauce thickens and turns dark brown, about 1 1/2 minutes. Transfer the mixture to a serving platter. Serve immediately accompanied by the rice.

Steak and Tomato Kabobs with Avocado Cream

JAMIE PURVIANCE/REPRINTED FROM *WEBER'S ART OF THE GRILL* (CHRONICLE)

1 teaspoon minced garlic
1 teaspoon dry mustard
2 teaspoons kosher salt, plus more to taste
1 teaspoon chili powder
$1/2$ teaspoon paprika
$1/2$ teaspoon ground coriander
$1/2$ teaspoon ground cumin
1 Hass avocado
One 2-inch piece English cucumber
$1/4$ cup sour cream

$1/4$ cup thinly sliced green onions
$1/4$ cup chopped fresh dill
3 to 4 dashes Tabasco sauce
Juice of 1 lime
$1/4$ cup water
2 pounds top sirloin
18 to 24 cherry tomatoes
Vegetable oil for brushing cooking grate
8 metal or wooden skewers (if wooden, soaked in water for 30 minutes)

✱ Preheat the grill to medium.

✱ In a medium bowl, mix together the garlic, mustard, 2 teaspoons salt, chili powder, paprika, coriander and cumin.

✱ Pit and peel the avocado and place it in a food processor or blender. Peel the cucumber and cut it into 1-inch dice. Add it to the processor or blender with the sour cream, green onions, dill, Tabasco, lime juice and water. Puree until smooth. Season with salt to taste. Pour the sauce into a small bowl, cover and refrigerate until ready to use (this can be made up to 1 day ahead). Bring to room temperature before serving.

✱ Cut the beef into 1½-inch pieces. Place them in a medium bowl and coat with the spice mixture (dry rub). Thread 3 tomatoes and 3 or 4 pieces of beef onto each skewer, separating the pieces of beef with tomatoes.

✱ Brush the cooking grate with vegetable oil. Grill the kabobs directly over medium heat, turning once, for 7 to 8 minutes total. The skin of the tomatoes should be lightly charred and starting to slip off. Serve warm with the avocado cream.

Montevidean Stuffed Beef Roll (Matambre)

STEVEN RAICHLEN/REPRINTED FROM *THE BARBECUE BIBLE* (WORKMAN)

1/2 large red bell pepper, stemmed and
  seeded
1/2 large green bell pepper, stemmed and
  seeded
One 6-ounce piece Romano cheese
One 6-ounce piece kielbasa sausage
2 large eggs, hard cooked, peeled and
  cooled (optional)
1 long carrot, peeled

6 slices bacon
1 beef flank steak (about 1 1/2 to 1 3/4
  pounds), butterflied
Salt and freshly ground black pepper
  to taste
1 teaspoon dried oregano
1/2 teaspoon dried sage
Chimichurri (*recipe follows*)

✳ Set the grill up for indirect cooking, placing a drip pan in the center. Preheat the grill to medium-low.

✳ Cut the peppers, cheese and sausage lengthwise into 1/2-inch-thick strips. Cut the eggs, if using, lengthwise into quarters. Cut the carrot lengthwise into quarters. Lay the bacon strips on a large (24-by-24-inch) square of heavy-duty aluminum foil, leaving a space of 1 inch between each; the strips should run parallel to the edge of the work surface. Place the butterflied flank steak on top of the bacon so that the grain of the meat (and the seam between the meat halves) runs perpendicular to the bacon.

✳ Season the meat generously with salt and pepper and sprinkle with the oregano and sage. Arrange strips of sausage in a neat row, end to end, along the edge of the meat closest to you. Place a row or red bell pepper strips next to it, then a row of cheese strips, then carrot strips, then green bell pepper strips, then hard-cooked eggs, if using. Repeat the process until all the ingredients are used. Leave the last 3 inches of meat uncovered.

✳ Starting at the edge closest to you and using the foil to help you, roll up the meat with the filling to make a compact roll. It's a lot like rolling a jelly roll. Pin the top edge shut with metal skewers or tie the roll with a few lengths of butcher's string. Encase the roll in the foil, twisting the ends to make what will look like a large sausage. Poke a few holes in the foil at each end to allow for the release of steam.

✳ When ready to cook, place the beef roll in the center of the grill, away from the fire. Cover the grill. Cook until very tender, 1 1/2 to 2 hours. (If using charcoal, add 10 to 12 fresh coals per side after 1 hour.) To test for doneness, insert a metal skewer right through the foil covering. It should pierce the meat easily and be piping hot to the touch when withdrawn. Transfer the beef roll to a cutting board and let cool for 15 minutes.

✳ Remove the foil and skewers or string, then cut the matambre crosswise into 1-inch slices to serve. Serve with the chimichurri.

(continued on next page)

SERVES 4

THIS RECIPE MAY SOUND COMPLICATED, BUT IT CAN BE ASSEMBLED IN fifteen MINUTES. IF DESIRED, YOU CAN ASK YOUR BUTCHER TO butterfly THE MEAT FOR YOU. CHIMICHURRI IS THE traditional ACCOMPANIMENT TO SOUTH AMERICAN GRILLED MEATS. NO TWO CHIMICHURRI RECIPES ARE exactly ALIKE, ALTHOUGH THE basic RECIPE CONTAINS JUST four INGREDIENTS: PARSLEY, GARLIC, OLIVE OIL AND SALT.

Chimichurri

1 bunch fresh Italian parsley, stemmed
1 small bulb garlic, broken into cloves and
    peeled (8 to 10 cloves in all)
1 medium carrot, peeled and grated on
    the coarse side of a grater
1 cup extra-virgin olive oil
$1/3$ cup white wine vinegar or distilled
    vinegar, or more to taste

$1/4$ cup water
1 teaspoon salt, or more to taste
1 teaspoon dried oregano
$1/2$ teaspoon crushed red pepper flakes, or
    more to taste
$1/2$ teaspoon freshly ground black pepper

✶ Combine the parsley and garlic in a food processor and pulse to chop as finely as possible.

✶ Add the carrot, oil, $1/3$ cup vinegar, water, salt, oregano, pepper flakes and black pepper. Process to mix. Taste for seasoning, adding vinegar, salt, or pepper flakes as necessary; the sauce should be highly seasoned. The chimichurri will keep for several days in the refrigerator (you may need to re-season it just before serving), but it tastes best served within a few hours of making. *Makes about 2 cups.*

Lisa's Lazy Pot Roast

BRUCE AIDELLS/REPRINTED FROM *THE COMPLETE MEAT COOKBOOK* **(HOUGHTON MIFFLIN)**

1 teaspoon dried thyme

1 tablespoon chopped fresh rosemary, or 1 teaspoon dried

1 tablespoon paprika

1 tablespoon kosher salt, plus more to taste

1 teaspoon freshly ground black pepper, plus more to taste

One boneless beef chuck roast or beef brisket (about 4 pounds), trimmed of most fat

2 tablespoons vegetable oil

1/2 cup water, or beef or chicken broth, or more if needed

5 cups thinly sliced onions (about 3 large onions)

6 cloves garlic, chopped

✽ Combine the herbs, paprika, 1 tablespoon salt and 1 teaspoon pepper in a small bowl. Rub the meat thoroughly with the mixture. You can cook the roast immediately, but it will taste better if it sits for an hour or two at room temperature, or overnight in a self-sealing plastic bag, or well wrapped, in the refrigerator.

✽ Preheat the oven to 350°F. In a large, heavy casserole or a Dutch oven, heat the vegetable oil over medium-high heat. Brown the meat on all sides, about 7 minutes. Remove and set aside. Pour off any fat from the pan and deglaze the pan with the water or broth, scraping up any browned bits with a wooden spoon or spatula. Put the roast back in the pan, cover it with the sliced onions and garlic, cover and bake for 1 hour.

✽ Remove the cover, turn the roast over so that it is on top of the onions and continue to cook, uncovered, for another hour, adding more liquid if needed. Stir the onions around after about 30 minutes so they can brown more evenly.

✽ Replace the cover and continue to cook for 1 hour more, or until the meat is fork-tender; brisket will take a little longer than chuck. Remove the meat from the pan and let it rest, covered loosely with foil, while you prepare the sauce. (At this point, you can refrigerate the pot roast for later reheating. Refrigerate the cooking liquid separately. To serve later, remove any congealed fat from the cooking liquid and strain it before using it to reheat the meat gently.)

✽ To serve, strain and defat the sauce. Taste for salt and pepper. Cut the meat into thick slices or separate it into chunks. Spoon some sauce and onions over each serving.

SERVES 6, WITH LEFTOVERS

OLD-FASHIONED POT ROAST, THE kind OUR moms USED TO MAKE, IS THE QUINTESSENTIAL comfort FOOD. THIS VERSION COMES FROM ONE OF BRUCE'S RECIPE TESTERS, LISA WEISS, AND, HE CLAIMS "IT MAKES THE best POT ROAST WE'VE TASTED SINCE Mom's."

SERVES 6

THIS distinctively NEAPOLITAN DISH, THERE CALLED BRACIOLE, FEATURES BEEF THAT IS enhanced AND TENDERIZED BY BEING COOKED IN A flavored LIQUID. THE LIQUID HERE IS TOMATO PUREE, WHICH IS MEANT TO BE enjoyed ALONG WITH THE MEAT.

Beef Rolls in Meat Sauce

ARTHUR SCHWARTZ/REPRINTED FROM *NAPLES AT TABLE* (HARPERCOLLINS)

Filling

3 tablespoons pine nuts

1/4 cups loosely packed, finely chopped fresh Italian parsley

1 tablespoon finely minced garlic

1/4 cup freshly grated Parmigiano-Reggiano cheese

1/3 cup raisins

2 1/2 pounds chuck or top round, cut into twelve 6-by-4-by-1/4-inch slices

Salt to taste

1/4 cup extra-virgin olive oil

1 small or 1/2 medium onion, halved and thinly sliced (about 1/2 cup)

1/2 cup red wine

Two 28-ounce cans peeled Italian tomatoes, crushed or run through a food mill

1 teaspoon salt

1/8 teaspoon crushed red pepper flakes

✱ In a small bowl, mix all the filling ingredients together.

✱ Place the meat slices on a work surface and season lightly with salt. On the bottom half of each slice, place a scant tablespoon of the filling. Roll up each slice starting from the filled bottom half. Tie each slice with kitchen string or secure with toothpicks.

✱ Place the beef rolls in a heavy bottomed 6- to 7-quart pot or flameproof casserole, along with the oil and the onion. Cook over medium-high heat, turning the rolls regularly with tongs, until the meat has lost its raw color and is starting to brown, about 10 minutes.

✱ Add the wine and continue cooking over medium-high heat for about 5 minutes longer, continuing to turn the rolls regularly. The liquid in the pan should mostly evaporate.

✱ Add the tomatoes, 1 teaspoon salt and pepper flakes. Stir well, then bring to a gentle simmer. Cook over the lowest possible heat so that the sauce barely bubbles. Stirring often, cook uncovered for 1 1/2 to 2 hours.

✱ Remove the beef rolls when tender. Either keep them warm in a covered dish, to serve as a second course, or cool and refrigerate for another meal. If desired, continue cooking the sauce over very low heat for 30 minutes or so, until it reaches a good consistency.

VARIATION: A combination of beef rolls and sausage is excellent. After the beef rolls have cooked in the tomatoes for about 30 minutes, add up to 1 pound (about 5 links) of sweet sausage, with fennel if desired. Remove the sausage with the beef rolls.

Fresh Brisket of Beef with Delicious Gravy

ALAN ROSEN / REPRINTED FROM *WELCOME TO JUNIOR'S!* (WILLIAM MORROW)

SERVES 6 TO 8

EVERY MORNING, ONE OF THE oversized OVENS IN THE JUNIOR'S DOWN-STAIRS KITCHEN IS BUSY ROASTING A GIANT-SIZED brisket OF BEEF. AND FOR GOOD REASON: THIS IS ONE OF JUNIOR'S blue-ribbon SPECIALTIES. HERE'S A VERSION FOR THE home KITCHEN. THE best PART: IT ROASTS IN THE OVEN FOR HOURS, ASKING FOR VERY little ATTENTION FROM YOU.

1 fresh brisket of beef, first cut (about 5 pounds)
2 tablespoons salt
1 teaspoon freshly ground white pepper
2 cups chopped carrots
6 large cloves garlic

Delicious Gravy
3 tablespoons fat skimmed from the drippings, or 3 tablespoons unsalted butter
6 cups strained pan drippings (save the vegetables, if you wish)
3 large cloves garlic, minced
3 tablespoons all-purpose flour

✳ Preheat the oven to 350°F.

✳ Rub the brisket with the salt and pepper and place it, fat-side up, in a roasting pan. Pour in enough water to come about ⅔ up the sides of the brisket. Sprinkle the carrots and garlic into the water around the roast.

✳ Roast the brisket, uncovered, until browned and tender, about 3 hours, spooning the pan drippings frequently over the meat. If necessary, add a little extra water during the cooking to keep the liquid at least halfway up the sides of the brisket. Transfer the meat to a serving platter; reserve the vegetables if desired.

✳ To make the gravy, skim off any fat from the drippings into a large skillet. You need 3 tablespoons of fat; if necessary, just add a little butter to equal this amount. Strain the drippings into a large heatproof measuring cup, reserving the vegetables for the gravy, if you wish.

✳ Heat the fat in the skillet over medium-high heat. Add the garlic and sauté until it begins to soften. Whisk in the flour and cook, stirring constantly, until the flour mixture bubbles all over, about 2 minutes. Gradually pour in the strained drippings and continue cooking and whisking until the gravy thickens. Remove the gravy from the heat and stir in the reserved vegetables, if you wish.

✳ To serve, slice the brisket on the diagonal, about ½-inch thick. Serve it hot with a generous helping of gravy ladled over the top.

Stuffed Breast of Veal with Askenazic Stuffing

SUSAN FRIEDLAND/REPRINTED FROM *SHABBAT SHALOM* (LITTLE, BROWN)

2 cups chopped onions
3 tablespoons olive or vegetable oil
1 cup chopped celery
1 cup chopped carrots
4 cups sliced mushrooms
5 cups cubed day-old French bread, crusts removed

2 eggs, lightly beaten
2 tablespoons schmalz or olive oil
Salt and freshly ground black pepper to taste
1/2 cup chopped fresh Italian parsley
1 veal breast (8 to 10 pounds trimmed weight)

✳ Preheat the oven to 400°F.

✳ In a large skillet, sauté the onions in 2 tablespoons of the oil over low heat for about 15 minutes, until very soft but not colored. Add the celery and carrots and sauté for an additional 10 minutes. With a slotted spoon, transfer the vegetables to a large bowl.

✳ Add the mushrooms to the skillet along with the remaining 1 tablespoon oil. Sauté them until they give up their liquid. Combine them with the other vegetables.

✳ Moisten the bread under running water. Squeeze the water out with your hands. Beat the bread into the vegetables with a wooden spoon, along with the eggs, schmalz or oil, salt, pepper and parsley; you'll have 4 to 4 1/2 cups of stuffing.

✳ Rub the veal breast inside and out with salt and pepper. Loosely fill the pocket of the veal breast with stuffing. (Put any leftover stuffing in an ovenproof dish; place it in the oven with the veal during the last hour of roasting, basting it with the pan juices from time to time.) Brush the outside of the breast with oil. Place the breast on a rack in a roasting pan, rib-side down. Roast it for 30 minutes; reduce the heat to 350°F and roast for an additional 2 to 2 1/2 hours, until the breast is brown and crisp. Remove it from the oven and let it rest for 15 minutes.

✳ To serve, remove the stuffing and transfer to a serving bowl. Slice the veal between the ribs. Combine in a serving bowl the stuffing from the veal with the stuffing cooked separately; serve warm.

SERVES 8

BREAST OF veal DOESN'T OFFER A LOT OF MEAT IN RELATION TO ITS WEIGHT AND SIZE. BUT IT'S A NATURAL FOR STUFFING AND satisfying TO EAT. ASK THE BUTCHER TO CUT A pocket IN THE VEAL BREAST AND TO CRACK THE BREAST BONE BETWEEN THE RIBS TO SIMPLIFY SLICING. Schmalz, FLAVORED RENDERED CHICKEN FAT, IS USED LIKE butter IN JEWISH HOUSEHOLDS.

Lamb Stew with Mixed Nut Pesto

GERALD HIRIGOYEN/REPRINTED FROM *THE BASQUE KITCHEN* **(HARPERCOLLINS)**

SERVES 4 TO 6

THE nut "PESTO" THAT
ADORNS THIS WONDERFUL
LAMB AND VEGETABLE STEW
IS best MADE WITH A
MORTAR AND PESTLE. THIS
METHOD IS SLOWER THAN
A food PROCESSOR, BUT
THE RESULT GIVES THE DISH
A MORE rustic TEXTURE
AND CHARACTER.

6 tablespoons olive oil
4 pounds boneless lamb shoulder, cut into
   1-inch cubes
1 medium leek, trimmed and cut into
   1/2-inch dice
1 medium onion, cut into 1/2-inch dice
1 medium carrot, cut into 1/2-inch dice
4 cups veal stock or canned low-sodium
   chicken broth
1 tablespoon kosher salt, or to taste

1/4 teaspoon freshly ground white pepper,
   or to taste
4 cloves garlic
1/3 cup hazelnuts
1/3 cup walnuts
1/3 cup almonds
2 teaspoons extra-virgin olive oil
2 tablespoons unsalted butter
2 tablespoons chopped fresh Italian parsley

✹ Warm 2 tablespoons of the olive oil in a large, heavy-bottomed saucepan over high heat. Working in two batches, add the lamb and sauté until it begins to brown, 2 to 3 minutes. Transfer the meat to a colander using a slotted spoon. Repeat with 2 more tablespoons of the olive oil and the remaining lamb.

✹ Add the leek, onion, carrot and remaining 2 tablespoons of the olive oil to the skillet and sauté for 2 to 3 minutes.

✹ Return the meat to the pan. Add the broth, salt and pepper, and bring to a boil. Reduce the heat to a simmer, cover, and cook, stirring occasionally, until the lamb is cooked through and very tender, about 50 minutes. Occasionally skim the top to remove any visible fat.

✹ Using a mortar and pestle, grind the garlic, hazelnuts, walnuts, almonds and extra-virgin olive oil into a chunky paste.

✹ Strain the cooking liquid from the lamb into a small saucepan. Transfer the meat to a deep serving platter and cover with aluminum foil to keep warm.

✹ Place the cooking liquid over high heat and cook until reduced by half, occasionally skimming the surface. Add the nut pesto and return to a boil. Reduce the heat and simmer for 5 minutes. Swirl in the butter until melted. Season with salt and pepper to taste.

✹ To serve, pour the sauce over the lamb and garnish with the parsley.

Barba Yianni's Grilled Lamb

BRUCE AIDELLS/REPRINTED FROM *THE COMPLETE MEAT COOKBOOK* **(HOUGHTON MIFFLIN)**

1/3 cup olive oil
Juice of 2 lemons
1/4 cup dried oregano, preferably Greek,
   or 1/2 cup chopped fresh
6 cloves garlic, chopped
1 teaspoon salt

1/2 teaspoon freshly ground black pepper
One 4 1/2-pound leg of lamb, fat trimmed,
   butterflied
Greek Grape Leaf and Mint Sauce (*recipe
   follows*)

✳ In a small bowl, mix the oil, lemon juice, oregano, garlic, salt and pepper into a paste and rub it all over the lamb. Place the lamb in a shallow bowl and cover with any remaining marinade. Marinate for about 2 hours at room temperature; or, preferably, cover the lamb and marinate overnight in the refrigerator, turning the meat from time to time.

✳ Grill the lamb over a medium-hot barbecue fire for about 5 minutes per side, until it registers 130° to 135°F on an instant-read thermometer for medium rare. Turn the lamb once or twice during grilling.

✳ Cut the lamb into serving slices and serve with the Greek grape leaf and mint sauce.

Greek Grape Leaf and Mint Sauce

1/3 cup chopped, bottled Greek grape
   leaves, stems removed
3 tablespoons chopped fresh mint, or
   2 tablespoons dried Greek oregano
2 teaspoons minced garlic
1 teaspoon salt
1 cup chopped fresh Italian parsley

1/4 cup fresh lemon juice
2 tablespoons chopped capers
1 tablespoon freshly ground black pepper
1/4 cup chopped green onions (white and
   green parts)
1 1/2 cups olive oil

✳ Blend or process all the ingredients in a blender or food processor. The sauce will keep refrigerated in a closed jar for 1 to 2 weeks. *Makes 2 to 3 cups.*

SERVES 6 TO 8

THE MARINADE IN THIS RECIPE works EQUALLY well WITH LAMB CHOPS, KEBABS OR BUTTERFLIED LEG OF lamb. YOU CAN ALSO USE IT ON PORK OR CHICKEN. TO SAVE TIME, ASK YOUR butcher TO BUTTERFLY THE LAMB.

Eggplant Stacks with Roasted Corn Vinaigrette

JAMIE PURVIANCE/REPRINTED FROM *WEBER'S ART OF THE GRILL* (CHRONICLE)

Vinaigrette
1 ear corn, unshucked
1 red bell pepper
2 tablespoons finely chopped shallots
2 tablespoons balsamic vinegar
2 tablespoons coarsely chopped fresh basil
5 tablespoons extra-virgin olive oil
8 medium tomato slices, each $1/4$-inch thick
Kosher salt and freshly ground pepper
    to taste

Eggplant
12 globe eggplant slices, each about
    4 inches in diameter and $1/2$-inch thick
Kosher salt for rubbing eggplant
Olive oil for brushing eggplant
Freshly ground black pepper to taste
$1/2$ cup grated or sliced Asiago cheese

✱ Preheat the grill to medium.

✱ To make the vinaigrette, soak the corn in water for 10 minutes. Grill the corn directly over medium heat, turning occasionally, until the husk is completely charred, 15 to 18 minutes. Remove and discard the charred husk and the inner silks. Remove the kernels with a sharp knife and place them in a medium bowl. Grill the bell pepper directly over medium heat, turning occasionally, until the skin is completely black and blistered, 10 to 12 minutes. Transfer the pepper to a paper bag, seal tightly and let cool for 15 minutes. Remove the pepper, discard the charred skin and seeds and finely dice. Add the bell pepper to the corn along with the shallots, vinegar, basil, olive oil and tomato slices. Season with salt and pepper. Make sure the tomatoes are covered by the vinaigrette.

✱ Meanwhile, rub both sides of the eggplant slices thoroughly with salt. Allow them to sit in a colander placed in the sink or over a plate for about 30 minutes to draw out the bitter juices. Rinse well and pat dry. Brush the eggplant thoroughly with olive oil and season with salt and pepper.

✱ Grill the eggplant slices directly over medium heat, turning once, until tender, about 10 to 12 minutes total.

✱ To assemble the stacks, start with an eggplant slice. Top with 1 tablespoon of the cheese and then a marinated tomato slice. Repeat the layers, ending with an eggplant slice. Carefully place the stacks on a small baking sheet. Place the baking sheet on the grill grate directly over medium heat and cook until the cheese melts, 2 to 3 minutes.

✱ Place the stacks on individual plates. Spoon the vinaigrette on top and around the sides. Serve warm.

DESSERTS

Grilled Peaches with Fresh Cherry Sauce

JAMIE PURVIANCE / REPRINTED FROM *WEBER'S ART OF THE GRILL* (CHRONICLE)

1 pound dark cherries, pitted (about 1 cup)
1 tablespoon granulated sugar
1/2 cup dry red wine
1 teaspoon balsamic vinegar
1 teaspoon kirsch (cherry liqueur)

4 medium peaches
2 tablespoons unsalted butter
2 tablespoons brown sugar
1 cup vanilla ice cream
4 cookies

✱ Preheat a gas or electric grill to medium.

✱ In a skillet over medium-high heat, combine the pitted cherries, granulated sugar, red wine and balsamic vinegar. Bring to a simmer and cook, stirring occasionally, until the fruit is soft, 6 to 8 minutes. Transfer the mixture to a food processor and puree until completely smooth. Return the mixture to the skillet over medium-high heat. Add the kirsch. Simmer until reduced to about 1/4 cup, 1 to 2 minutes.

✱ Cut the peaches in half and remove and discard the pits. Place the peach halves in a medium bowl.

✱ In a small saucepan set over low heat, melt the butter and brown sugar together. Pour the butter mixture into the bowl with the peaches and toss to coat well.

✱ Grill the peaches over direct heat, turning once, until grill marks are clearly visible and the peaches are soft, 10 to 12 minutes total.

✱ While the peaches are still warm, layer in each of 4 serving glasses 2 peach halves, 1 scoop of ice cream and 1 tablespoon of the cherry sauce. Tuck a cookie into each glass and serve immediately.

SERVES 4

GRILLING FRUITS, SUCH AS THESE succulent PEACHES, BRINGS OUT AND caramelizes THEIR NATURAL SUGARS, WHILE IMPARTING AN INTRIGUING smoky HINT TO THEIR FLESH. HERE IS A twist ON THE classic SUMMER- TIME DISH, PEACH MELBA.

Peaches in Paradise

BILL HUFNAGLE/REPRINTED FROM *BIKER BILLY'S FREEWAY-A-FIRE* (WILLIAM MORROW)

Crumb Topping
1/2 cup firmly packed light brown sugar
1/3 cup all-purpose flour
1/4 teaspoon ground cayenne pepper
1/2 teaspoon ground cinnamon
1/4 teaspoon ground nutmeg
4 tablespoons (1/2 stick) butter, cut into
  4 pieces

Peaches
1 fresh habanero chile, stemmed and
  seeded
Two 16-ounce cans sliced peaches in light
  syrup, drained, liquid reserved

1/2 cup honey
2 tablespoons cornstarch
1/4 teaspoon ground cinnamon
1/4 teaspoon ground nutmeg
1 1/2 teaspoons fresh lemon juice

Biscuit Batter
1 cup all-purpose flour
1/2 teaspoon salt
1 tablespoon sugar
1 1/2 teaspoons baking powder
2 tablespoons butter
1/2 cup milk

✱ To make the crumb topping, combine the brown sugar, flour, cayenne, cinnamon and nutmeg in the workbowl of a food processor. Pulse 2 or 3 times to mix completely. Add the butter, arranging the pieces evenly around the workbowl. Process until the butter is cut into the flour, creating a granular texture, 1 to 2 minutes. Set aside.

✱ To prepare the peaches, combine the habanero chile, reserved peach syrup, honey, cornstarch, cinnamon, nutmeg and lemon juice in a small saucepan. Stir well, place over medium-high heat and bring to a boil. Boil for 2 minutes, stirring constantly, until the sauce begins to thicken. Remove the saucepan from the heat. Remove and discard the habanero chile.

✱ Preheat the oven to 400°F. To make the biscuit batter, combine the flour, salt, sugar and baking powder in the workbowl of a food processor. Pulse 2 or 3 times to mix completely. Add the butter, arranging the pieces evenly around the workbowl. Process until the butter is cut into the flour, creating a granular texture, 1 to 2 minutes. While the blades are spinning, pour in the milk and process until a dough forms and begins to move around the bowl as a ball, approximately 1 minute.

✱ To assemble, place the sliced peaches in an 8-inch square baking pan. Pour the sauce over the peaches and stir to coat the peaches evenly with the sauce. Spoon the biscuit batter on top of the peaches (you want to distribute the biscuit batter evenly, but not to form a crust or completely cover the peaches). Sprinkle on the crumb topping. Bake until the top is golden brown, 30 to 35 minutes. Let cool for 10 minutes before serving.

Grilled Sugar-Dipped Pineapple

STEVEN RAICHLEN / REPRINTED FROM *THE BARBECUE BIBLE* (WORKMAN)

1 ripe pineapple
8 tablespoons (1 stick) unsalted butter,
    melted
3/4 cup sugar

1 teaspoon grated lime zest
1 teaspoon ground cinnamon
1/8 teaspoon ground cloves
1/2 cup dark rum, for flambéing (optional)

✴ Preheat the grill to high.

✴ Cut the leafy top off the pineapple, then cut off the rind. Slice the fruit into 8 or 10 even rounds. Using a pineapple corer or paring knife, remove the core from each round.

✴ When ready to cook, place the melted butter in a shallow bowl; combine the sugar, lime zest, cinnamon and cloves in a separate bowl. Bring both bowls to the grillside. Oil the grill grates. Dip each slice of pineapple first in melted butter, then in the sugar mixture, shaking off the excess. Arrange the pineapple slices on the hot grate and grill, turning with tongs, until browned and sizzling, 5 to 8 minutes per side. Transfer the pineapple slices to plates or a platter, arranging the slices in an overlapping fashion.

✴ If using the rum, warm it in a small saucepan on one side of the grill; do not let it boil or even become hot. Remove it from the heat and then, making sure your sleeves are rolled up and hair is tied back, light a long match and use it to ignite the rum, averting your face as you do so. Very carefully pour the flaming rum over the pineapple and serve it immediately.

SERVES 8 TO 10

PINEAPPLES taste PARTICULARLY good GRILLED, THE CHARRED FLAVOR MESHING NICELY WITH THE CARAMELIZED sweetness OF THE FRUIT. WHEN BUYING PINEAPPLE, LOOK FOR FRUIT WITH A golden RIND. IT WILL BE JUICIER AND SWEETER THAN THE USUAL GREEN-RIND PINEAPPLES.

Fire-Grilled Banana Split

STEVEN RAICHLEN/REPRINTED FROM *THE BARBECUE BIBLE* (WORKMAN)

SERVES 4

FOR THIS UNUSUAL
TAKE ON THE classic
SODA FOUNTAIN DESSERT,
THE bananas ARE FIRST
GRILLED WITH A COATING
OF maple syrup AND
DARK RUM, THEN PAIRED
WITH TROPICAL-FLAVORED
COCONUT ICE CREAM AND
macadamia NUTS.

1 cup maple syrup
1/2 cup dark rum
1/4 cup sugar
1/2 teaspoon ground cinnamon
1/4 teaspoon freshly grated nutmeg
4 slightly green bananas

1 quart good-quality coconut ice cream
2 cups whipped cream
1/4 cup shredded coconut, toasted
2 tablespoons chopped macadamia nuts, toasted

✳ Preheat the grill to high.

✳ Combine the syrup, rum, sugar, cinnamon and nutmeg in a large bowl and whisk until the sugar is dissolved. Set aside to cool.

✳ When ready to cook, oil the grill grate. Arrange the bananas on the hot grate and grill, turning with tongs, until nicely browned all over, 6 to 8 minutes in all. Transfer the bananas to a cutting board and slice on the diagonal into bite-sized pieces. Stir the hot bananas into the syrup mixture and allow to cool to room temperature. Cover and let marinate, in the refrigerator, for 3 hours.

✳ To prepare the banana splits, mound 1/4 of the ice cream in the center of each of 4 shallow dessert bowls. Spoon the bananas with a little syrup mixture over the ice cream. Spoon or pipe rosettes of whipped cream on top and sprinkle with toasted coconut and macadamia nuts. Serve immediately.

Walnut Cake

COLMAN ANDREWS/REPRINTED FROM *SAVEUR COOKS AUTHENTIC FRENCH* (CHRONICLE)

1/2 cup chopped walnuts
3 eggs
1 cup sugar
1/3 cup walnut oil
1/3 cup dry white wine

1 1/2 cups flour
2 teaspoons baking powder
1/8 teaspoon salt
Walnut liqueur or vanilla ice cream for
    accompaniment

✳ Preheat the oven to 350°F. Generously grease a 9-inch cake pan.

✳ Place the walnuts in a small dry saucepan and cook over medium heat, shaking the pan, until the nuts are lightly toasted, 5 to 10 minutes. Set aside.

✳ Beat the eggs in a medium bowl with an electric mixer. Gradually add the sugar and beat until the mixture is light and fluffy. Add the walnut oil and wine and mix well. The batter will be quite thick.

✳ Sift together the flour, baking powder, and salt into a large bowl. Add the egg mixture to the flour mixture and mix with a wooden spoon until the ingredients are just combined. Gently fold in the nuts, then spoon the batter into the pan.

✳ Bake the cake until a toothpick can be inserted and pulled out clean, about 40 minutes. Remove the cake from the oven, cool for 10 minutes, and then turn it out onto a cooling rack. Allow the cake to cool completely, then serve it cut into wedges drizzled with walnut liqueur, or accompanied by vanilla ice cream.

SERVES 8

CHOPPED WALNUTS AND WALNUT OIL infuse THIS SIMPLE cake, TYPICAL OF WHAT YOU MIGHT SEE IN FRENCH bakery windows ON THE STREETS OF PARIS.

Rice Pudding Cake

MICHAEL ROBERTS / REPRINTED FROM *PARISIAN HOME COOKING* **(WILLIAM MORROW)**

2 tablespoons plus 1 teaspoon unsalted
  butter
2/3 cup Arborio rice
1 quart whole milk
1/2 teaspoon freshly grated nutmeg
1/8 teaspoon ground cinnamon
1/2 teaspoon vanilla extract

Grated zest of 3 lemons
3/4 cup sugar
3 large eggs, beaten
3 tablespoons water
Crème fraîche or whipped cream for
  accompaniment

✳ Preheat the oven to 350°F. Butter a 7- to 8-inch 2-inch-deep round cake pan with 1 teaspoon of the butter and set aside.

✳ Combine the remaining 2 tablespoons butter, the rice, milk, nutmeg, cinnamon, vanilla, lemon zest, and ½ cup of the sugar in a 2-quart pot, place over medium heat, and cook for 15 minutes. (If the contents of the pot come to a full boil, lower the heat to keep the milk at a low simmer.) Remove from the heat and let the mixture cool for 10 minutes. Beat in the eggs and set aside.

✳ Combine the remaining ¼ cup sugar and the water in a small saucepan, place over medium-high heat, and cook until the sugar melts and turns a dark caramel color. Immediately pour the caramel into the center of the prepared cake pan. Do not worry if it doesn't cover the bottom of the pan, as it will dissolve and spread during baking.

✳ Pour the rice mixture into the cake pan and give it a few gentle shakes to distribute the rice evenly. Carefully transfer the cake pan to the top rack of the oven and bake for 35 to 40 minutes, or until the surface shows some golden areas and the center is just set. Remove the cake pan from the oven and let cool to room temperature.

✳ To unmold, place a plate over the cake pan and invert the plate and pan. Give a few gentle taps to the bottom of the cake pan and carefully remove it from the cake. Place another plate over the cake and invert the plates to turn the cake right-side up again. Serve the cake warm or at room temperature and accompany with crème fraîche or whipped cream.

Lemon Poppy Seed Pound Cake

ROSE LEVY BERANBAUM/REPRINTED FROM *THE CAKE BIBLE* (WILLIAM MORROW)

3 tablespoons milk
3 large eggs
1 1/2 teaspoons vanilla extract
1 1/2 cups sifted cake flour
3/4 cup sugar
3/4 teaspoon baking powder
1/4 teaspoon salt

1 tablespoon loosely packed grated lemon zest
3 tablespoons poppy seeds
13 tablespoons unsalted butter (1 5/8 sticks), softened

Lemon Syrup
1/4 cup plus 2 tablespoons sugar
1/4 cup freshly squeezed lemon juice

✱ Preheat the oven to 350°F. Grease and flour one 8-by-4-by-2 1/2-inch loaf pan, or a 6-cup loaf or fluted tube pan.

✱ In a medium mixing bowl, lightly mix the milk, eggs and vanilla.

✱ In a large mixing bowl, combine the dry ingredients, including the lemon zest and poppy seeds, and mix with a mixer on low speed for 30 seconds to blend. Add the butter and 1/2 of the egg mixture. Mix on low speed until the dry ingredients are moistened. Increase to medium speed (high speed if using a hand mixer) and beat for 1 minute to aerate and develop the cake's structure.

✱ Scrape down the sides of the bowl. Gradually add the remaining egg mixture in 2 batches, beating for 20 seconds after each addition to incorporate the ingredients and strengthen the structure. Scrape down the sides of the bowl.

✱ Scrape the batter into the prepared pan and smooth the surface with a spatula. The batter will be almost 1/2 inch from the top of the loaf pan. (If your pan is slightly smaller, use any excess batter for cupcakes.) Bake for 55 to 65 minutes (35 to 45 minutes in a fluted tube pan) or until a wooden toothpick inserted in the center comes out clean. Cover loosely with buttered foil after 30 minutes to prevent overbrowning. *The cake should start to shrink from the sides of the pan only after removal from the oven.*

✱ Shortly before the cake is done, prepare the lemon syrup: In a small pan over medium heat, stir the sugar and lemon juice until dissolved. As soon as the cake comes out of the oven, place the pan on a rack, poke the cake all over with a wire tester, and brush it with 1/2 of the syrup. Cool in the pan for 10 minutes. Loosen the sides with a spatula and invert onto a greased wire rack. Poke the bottom of the cake with the wire tester, brush it with some syrup, and reinvert onto a greased wire rack. Brush the sides with the remaining syrup and let cool before wrapping airtight. Store for 24 hours before eating to give the syrup a chance to distribute evenly.

SERVES 8

THE fresh, LIGHT FLAVOR OF LEMON BLENDS beautifully WITH THE BUTTERY FLAVOR OF POUND CAKE. THE LEMON SYRUP TENDERIZES, ADDS tartness AND HELPS TO KEEP THE CAKE FRESH FOR A FEW DAYS LONGER THAT USUAL. POPPY SEEDS ADD A delightful CRUNCH.

Lemon Sponge Pudding Cake with Fresh Berries

JAMES MCNAIR/REPRINTED FROM *JAMES MCNAIR'S FAVORITES* **(CHRONICLE)**

¹/₄ cup (¹/₂ stick) unsalted butter, at room temperature, plus more for greasing pan

1 cup sugar

2 teaspoons finely grated or minced lemon zest

3 eggs, at room temperature, separated and yolks lightly beaten

¹/₄ cup all-purpose flour

Pinch of salt

1¹/₄ cups milk (not fat-free)

¹/₂ cup freshly squeezed lemon juice

Seasonal berries for accompaniment

✱ Position racks so that the cake will bake in the middle of the oven and preheat the oven to 350°F. With a pastry brush, generously grease an 8-inch square pan or a 1½-quart baking dish with butter and set aside.

✱ In a bowl, combine the sugar, ¼ cup butter and lemon zest and beat with an electric mixer at medium speed until creamy, about 3 minutes. With the mixer still running, slowly drizzle in the egg yolks and beat well. Stir in the flour, salt, milk and lemon juice. Set the mixture aside.

✱ In a stainless steel bowl with clean beaters, beat the egg whites at medium speed until they form peaks that are stiff, but still moist when the beater is raised. Stir about ¼ of the whites into the batter to lighten it. Using a rubber spatula, fold in the remaining whites. Pour the mixture into the prepared baking pan.

✱ Place the pudding container on a rack set in a large, deep baking pan. Transfer the pan to the oven and pour enough hot (not boiling) water into the large pan to reach about half-way up the sides of the pudding container. Bake until the top pudding layer is set and lightly browned, about 45 minutes. Regulate the oven temperature during baking to maintain water at the almost simmering stage; do not allow it to boil.

✱ Remove the pudding container from the water bath and place it on a wire rack to cool slightly, then serve it warm with the berries.

SERVES 6

HERE'S AN OLD-TIME pudding CAKE THAT SEPARATES DURING BAK-ING INTO spongy CAKE crowning A CREAMY SAUCE. SERVE IT EITHER CHILLED OR WARM FROM THE oven.

Lemon-Scented White Cake
with Milk Chocolate Frosting

NICK MALGIERI/REPRINTED FROM *CHOCOLATE* (HARPERCOLLINS)

Lemony White Cake

2¹/₄ cups cake flour

4 teaspoons baking powder

¹/₂ teaspoon salt

8 tablespoons (1 stick) unsalted butter, softened

1¹/₂ cups sugar

2 teaspoons finely grated lemon zest

¹/₂ teaspoon lemon extract

¹/₂ cup egg whites (from about 4 large eggs)

1³/₄ cups milk

Milk Chocolate Ganache

Zest of 2 lemons (removed in long strips with a vegetable peeler)

2 cups heavy cream

4 tablespoons (¹/₂ stick) unsalted butter, softened

20 ounces milk chocolate, cut into ¹/₄-inch pieces

✳ Set a rack at the middle level of the oven and preheat it to 350°F. Butter two 9-inch round cake pans (1½ to 2 inches deep) and line with parchment or waxed paper.

✳ Sift the cake flour, baking powder and salt onto a piece of parchment or waxed paper and set aside.

✳ With an electric mixer on medium speed, mix the butter and sugar until light, about 3 minutes. Mix in the lemon zest and extract.

✳ In a bowl, whisk together the egg whites and the milk.

✳ Add ⅓ of the flour mixture to the butter-sugar mixture and beat until smooth. Scrape down the bowl and beaters. Beat in ½ of the milk/egg white mixture until incorporated, then beat in another ⅓ of the flour mixture. Scrape down the bowl and beaters. Beat in the remaining liquid until it is absorbed, followed by the remaining flour mixture. Scrape well after each addition.

✳ Divide the batter between the prepared pans and smooth the tops evenly. Bake for about 30 to 35 minutes, until well risen and a toothpick inserted in the center emerges clean. Cool the cake layers in their pans for 5 minutes, then invert the layers onto racks to cool. Peel off the paper. If prepared in advance, double-wrap the layers in plastic wrap and chill for up to several days or freeze.

(continued on next page)

THE UNUSUAL FLAVORING FOR THIS CAKE IS lemon zest. IT IS USED IN BOTH THE LIGHT, MOIST CAKE AND THE MILK CHOCOLATE GANACHE AND IT DELICATELY perfumes AND COMPLEMENTS BOTH. IT works BECAUSE THE LEMON ZEST, WHICH IS RICH IN THE essential OIL OF LEMON, TRANSMITS A lemon PERFUME WITHOUT ANY OF THE ACIDITY OF LEMON JUICE, WHICH WOULD MAR THE chocolate FLAVOR.

✷ To make the ganache, place the pieces of zest in a saucepan and add the cream. Place over low heat and bring to a simmer. Remove from the heat and allow to steep for about 5 minutes. Remove the zests from the cream with a slotted spoon and discard them. Add the butter to the cream and bring to a boil over low heat. Remove from the heat and add the chocolate. Shake the pan to submerge the chocolate and allow it to stand for 5 minutes. Whisk smooth, then cool to room temperature. The ganache will thicken to spreading consistency.

✷ To finish the cake, place one cake layer right-side up on a platter or circle of cardboard. Place the ganache in a mixer bowl and beat until light, about 20 seconds. Using an offset spatula, spread the cake layer with a little more than ⅓ of the ganache. Place the other cake layer upside down on the ganache, so the smooth bottom of the cake layer is uppermost. Spread the top and sides of the cake evenly with most of the remaining ganache.

✷ Keep the cake at a cool room temperature before serving. Keep the leftovers under a cake dome at a cool room temperature or covered with plastic wrap in the refrigerator. Cut into wedges to serve.

Chocolate Domingo Cake

ROSE LEVY BERANBAUM / REPRINTED FROM *THE CAKE BIBLE* (WILLIAM MORROW)

¹/₄ cup plus 3 tablespoons Dutch processed unsweetened cocoa powder	1 cup sugar
²/₃ cup sour cream	³/₄ teaspoon baking powder
2 large eggs	¹/₄ teaspoon baking soda
1¹/₂ teaspoons vanilla extract	¹/₂ teaspoon salt
1¹/₂ cups plus 1 tablespoon sifted cake flour	14 tablespoons unsalted butter (1³/₄ sticks), softened

❋ Preheat the oven to 350°F. Grease a 9-by-2-inch cake pan or a 9-inch springform pan and line it with parchment or waxed paper. Grease the pan again and flour it.

❋ In a medium bowl, whisk together the cocoa, sour cream, eggs and vanilla until smooth.

❋ In a large bowl, combine all the remaining dry ingredients and mix with a mixer on low speed for 30 seconds to blend. Add the butter and ½ of the cocoa mixture. Mix on low speed until the ingredients are moistened. Increase to medium speed (high speed if using a hand mixer) and beat for 1½ minutes to aerate and develop the cake's structure. Scrape down the sides of the bowl. Gradually add the remaining cocoa mixture in 2 batches, beating for 20 seconds after each addition to incorporate the ingredients and strengthen the structure. Scrape down the sides of the bowl.

❋ Scrape the batter into the prepared pan and smooth the surface with a spatula. The pan will be about half full. Bake for 30 to 40 minutes, or until a tester inserted near the center comes out clean and the cake springs back when pressed lightly in the center. *The cake should start to shrink from the sides of the pan only after removal form the oven.*

❋ Let the cake cool in the pan on a rack for 10 minutes. Loosen the sides with a small metal spatula and invert onto a greased wire rack. Reinvert so that the top is up and cool completely before wrapping airtight. Cut into wedges to serve.

SERVES 10 TO 12

IN THE ancient TRADITION OF CREATING A FABULOUS RECIPE FOR A favorite OPERA STAR, ROSE NAMED THIS CAKE FOR HERS: PLACIDO DOMINGO, IN gratitude FOR THE PLEASURE OF HIS INCOMPARABLE PERFORMANCES.

Chocolate Polenta Pudding Cake

LYNNE ROSSETTO KASPER/REPRINTED FROM *THE ITALIAN COUNTRY TABLE* (SCRIBNER)

MAKES ONE 8-INCH
CAKE; SERVES 8 TO 10

COARSELY GROUND CORN-
MEAL AND top-quality
CHOCOLATE FORM THE
BASE OF THIS luscious,
MOIST CAKE. IT'S DELI-
CIOUS SERVED WITH THICK
SWEETENED cream, BUT
IS ALSO GOOD UNADORNED,
warm OR AT ROOM
TEMPERATURE.

2 1/2 cups whole milk
2/3 cup coarsely ground cornmeal
1/2 cup plus 4 tablespoons granulated
    sugar
1/2 teaspoon salt
8 ounces bittersweet chocolate, such as
    Lindt Excellence, Valrhona Grand Cru
    or Callebaut bittersweet
Grated zest of 1/2 large orange
1 1/2 teaspoons ground cinnamon

Generous 1/8 teaspoon freshly ground
    black pepper
4 large eggs, separated
1 tablespoon vanilla extract
1/2 cup heavy cream
1 tablespoon unsweetened cocoa powder
1 cup heavy cream (optional)
1 tablespoon granulated sugar (optional)
Confectioners' sugar for dusting

✴ In a 2-quart saucepan, bring the milk to a boil. Meanwhile, combine the cornmeal, 1/2 cup sugar and the salt in a medium stainless steel bowl. Whisk in the hot milk until smooth.

✴ Wash out the saucepan, fill it 2/3-full with water, and bring it to a simmer. Cover the bowl with foil, set it over the water and cook for 40 minutes; the polenta will be thick and stiff. Stir 3 or 4 times as it cooks and add water to the pan if necessary.

✴ Meanwhile, preheat the oven to 350°F. Butter an 8-inch springform pan. Finely chop 3/4 of the chocolate and cut the rest into generous 1-inch pieces.

✴ When the polenta is cooked, remove the bowl from the water. Blend in the finely chopped chocolate, the orange zest, cinnamon, pepper, egg yolks and vanilla. Place 1 cup of this mixture in another bowl and stir the cream into it. Set aside.

✴ In a large bowl, whip the egg whites until frothy. Beat in 3 tablespoons of the sugar, then whip to soft peaks. Fold 1/4 of the whites into the non-cream chocolate-polenta mixture to lighten it. Then fold in the rest, leaving a few white streaks. Fold in the chocolate chunks with one or two strokes.

✴ Pour 1/2 of the batter into the prepared pan. Using a spoon, hollow out the center of the batter so the polenta-cream mixture will sit in a pocket, and add the cream mixture. Cover with the rest of the batter. Sift the cocoa over the top, then sprinkle with the remaining 1 tablespoon granulated sugar.

✴ Bake for 1 hour, or until a knife inserted at the edge of the pudding comes out with moist crumbs on it, but when put into the center, comes out with cream streaks. Cool on a rack for 15 minutes.

✴ Meanwhile, if desired, whip the optional cream with the sugar until just thickened. Release the sides of the pan and set the cake on a plate. Serve warm or at room temperature, dusted with confectioners' sugar. Spoon some of the cream beside each slice, if desired.

Apple Wrapover

MARY CORPENING BARBER AND SARA CORPENING WHITEFORD / REPRINTED FROM *WRAPS* (CHRONICLE)

1/4 cup maple syrup
2 tablespoons dark rum
2 tablespoons butter
1 teaspoon fresh lemon juice
1 teaspoon ground cinnamon
Pinch of kosher salt

4 cups peeled, cored and diced apples
   (1/2-inch dice)
1/3 cup crème fraîche
Four 8-inch flour tortillas
1 tablespoon butter, melted (optional)
2 teaspoons sugar (optional)

✳ Combine the syrup, rum, butter, lemon juice, cinnamon and salt in a large nonstick skillet. Heat over high heat until the mixture begins to bubble. Add the apples and cook until tender, about 10 minutes. Add the crème fraîche and cook until the liquid is thick, about 2 minutes. Divide the filling among the tortillas and fold in the sides of each tortilla. Fold up the bottom of each tortilla and continue to roll up into a cylinder, enclosing the filling. Cut the wraps in half on the diagonal and serve.

✳ For a baked version, preheat the oven to 375°F. Line a baking sheet with aluminum foil and place the wraps (before cutting) seam-side down on the baking sheet. Brush with the melted butter and sprinkle with the sugar. Bake until the crust is crispy, about 30 minutes. Be certain there are no holes or tears in the tortilla before baking or all of the juices will escape, leaving you with a messy cluster of dried fruit.

SERVES 4

WRAPS NEED NOT ALWAYS BE STUFFED WITH savory FILLINGS. HERE TRADITIONAL AMERICAN APPLE PIE INGREDIENTS FILL THE tortillas AND ARE SERVED AS AN INNOVATIVE dessert.

Warm Butternut Cheesecake with Lime-Poached Cranberries

JIM COLEMAN/REPRINTED FROM *THE RITTENHOUSE COOKBOOK* **(TEN SPEED)**

1 cup peeled butternut squash cubes
   (1-inch cubes)
Yogurt Cheese (*recipe follows*)
1/4 cup brown sugar
1/4 cup granulated sugar
1/3 cup nonfat sour cream
1 cup egg substitute, such as Egg Beaters
1/4 teaspoon almond extract
Pinch of freshly grated nutmeg

Lime-Poached Cranberries
1/4 cup water
1/4 cup granulated sugar
1/4 cup pure maple syrup
1 cup fresh or frozen cranberries
Juice and minced zest of 1 lime

✳ Preheat the oven to 325°F. Coat a 6-inch cake pan with nonstick cooking spray.

✳ Bring a saucepan of water to a boil. Add the squash and poach for 10 to 15 minutes, or until tender. Transfer the squash to a food processor and puree until smooth. Add the yogurt cheese, brown and granulated sugars, sour cream, egg substitute, almond extract and nutmeg and pulse until the mixture is well combined and thoroughly smooth.

✳ Pour the batter into the prepared pan. Place the cake pan in a larger roasting pan. Place the pans in the oven and pour enough hot water in the larger pan to reach halfway up the sides of the cake pan. Bake for about 45 minutes, or until a knife inserted into the center comes out clean. Remove the cake from the oven and water bath and let cool for 1 hour before unmolding.

✳ Meanwhile, to prepare the cranberries, combine the water, sugar and maple syrup in a small saucepan and bring to a boil. Stir in the cranberries and cook over medium heat until the first cranberry begins to burst, about 5 or 6 minutes. Remove the pan from the heat, stir in the lime juice and zest, and let stand for 1 hour.

✳ Reduce the oven temperature to 200°F.

✳ Invert the cheesecake on a plate and tap lightly to remove from the pan. Cut the cheesecake into 6 pieces and place on ovenproof serving pates. Place the plates in the oven and heat just until warm, about 2 minutes. Remove from the oven, spoon the poached cranberries around the cheesecake slices and serve immediately.

Yogurt Cheese

2 cups nonfat, gelatin-free yogurt cheese

✳ Set a mesh sieve over a medium bowl and line the sieve with 2 layers of cheesecloth. Pour the yogurt into the sieve. Cover with plastic wrap and refrigerate overnight. Discard the liquid from the bowl. *Makes 1 cup.*

SERVES 6

THE BUTTERNUT SQUASH puree USED FOR THIS VERSION OF CHEESECAKE HAS A MORE delicate FLAVOR THAN THE MORE USUAL pumpkin, AND ALLOWS FOR A more SUBTLE PAIRING OF SPICES AND SEASONINGS. USING NONFAT YOGURT CHEESE AND SOUR CREAM, AS WELL AS EGG SUBSTITUE, MAKE THIS luscious DESSERT A HEALTHY INDULGENCE.

MAKES ABOUT 1 QUART

ANY variety OF FRESH

PEAR WILL WORK FOR THIS

SORBET. CHOOSE PEARS

THAT ARE fragrant

AND SLIGHTLY SOFT. IN

FACT, THE SOFTER THE

PEAR, THE better—AS

LONG (OF COURSE) AS IT

HASN'T SPOILED.

Pear Sorbet

BRUCE WEINSTEIN/REPRINTED FROM *THE ULTIMATE ICE CREAM BOOK* (WILLIAM MORROW)

3/4 cup plus 1 tablespoon sugar
2/3 cup water
1 1/2 pounds ripe pears (3 to 4 medium)

Juice of 1 lemon
1/2 teaspoon salt

✳ Combine the sugar and water in a small saucepan and place over low heat. Stir until the sugar dissolves completely. Raise the heat and boil the syrup for 1 minute. Remove from the heat and let the syrup to cool to room temperature.

✳ Peel the pears and remove the cores. Cut the pears into small pieces and place in a blender with the cooled sugar syrup, lemon juice and salt. Blend on low until the mixture is smooth. Refrigerate for at least 1 hour.

✳ Stir the chilled mixture, then freeze it in your ice cream machine according to the manufacturer's instructions. When finished, the sorbet will be soft but ready to eat. For firmer sorbet, transfer it to a freezer-safe container and freeze for at least 2 hours.

Variations

Red Wine-Pear Sorbet

✳ Substitute a hearty red wine, such as Cabernet Sauvignon or Zinfandel, for the water. Proceed with the recipe as directed.

Lemon-Pear Sorbet

✳ Increase the lemon juice to 1/4 cup. Add the grated zest of 1 lemon to the blender along with the pears. Proceed with the recipe as directed.

Pear-Ginseng Sorbet

✳ Add one 10ml vial of ginseng extract to the blender along with the pears. Proceed with the recipe as directed. (Check your local health food store for ginseng extract.)

Pear-Nutmeg Sorbet

✳ Add 1/2 teaspoon freshly ground nutmeg to the blender along with the pears. Proceed with the recipe as directed.

Vanilla Ice Cream, Philadelphia Style

BRUCE WEINSTEIN / REPRINTED FROM *THE ULTIMATE ICE CREAM BOOK* (WILLIAM MORROW)

3 cups heavy cream

³/4 cup plus 2 tablespoons sugar

2 teaspoons vanilla extract

✳ Heat the cream in a large heavy saucepan over medium heat until small bubbles appear around the edge. Do no let the cream boil. Remove from the heat and add the sugar, stirring until the sugar is completely dissolved. Allow the cream to cool slightly, then stir in the vanilla. Cover and refrigerate until cold, or overnight.

✳ Freeze in 1 or 2 batches in your ice cream machine according to the manufacturer's instructions. When finished, the ice cream will be soft, but ready to eat. For firmer ice cream, transfer it to a freezer-safe container and freeze for at least 2 hours.

Variations

Vanilla-Candy Bar Ice Cream

✳ Add 2 chopped candy bars of your choice to the machine when the ice cream is semifrozen. Allow the machine to mix in the candy. Proceed with the recipe as directed.

Vanilla-Candy Dish Ice Cream

✳ Add ½ cup small candies of your choice to the machine when the ice cream is semifrozen. Allow the machine to mix in the candy. Proceed with the recipe as directed.

Vanilla-Cracker Jack Ice Cream

✳ Add 1 cup crunchy caramel corn to the machine when the ice cream is semifrozen. Allow the machine to mix in the corn. Proceed with the recipe as directed.

MAKES ABOUT 1 QUART

THIS IS ONE OF THE OLDEST ways TO MAKE ICE CREAM AND STILL ONE OF THE easiest. ALL IT TAKES IS THREE INGREDI-ENTS. HEATING THE CREAM BEFORE ADDING THE SUGAR makes THE ICE CREAM SMOOTHER AND richer THAN NOT DOING SO.

Banana Sorbet

SUSAN FRIEDLAND/REPRINTED FROM *SHABBAT SHALOM* **(LITTLE, BROWN)**

4 overripe bananas

1/2 cup cold water

1/2 cup sugar

3 tablespoons fresh lemon juice

✳ Peel and slice the bananas. Puree them with the water in a food processor or blender until smooth. Add the sugar and lemon juice and process just to combine. Pour the mixture into a bowl and refrigerate for a minimum of 3 hours and up to 3 days.

✳ Whisk the mixture and pour it into the canister of an ice cream maker. Follow the manufacturer's instructions for freezing. When the sorbet is thick, transfer it to a serving dish if you are eating right away, or pack it into a plastic container for freezer storage. Place the sorbet in the freezer for 10 to 15 minutes before serving.

Fig Ice Cream

BRUCE WEINSTEIN/REPRINTED FROM *THE ULTIMATE ICE CREAM BOOK* **(WILLIAM MORROW)**

8 dried figs

2 large eggs

1 1/2 cups milk

1/2 cup sugar

1 cup heavy cream

1/2 teaspoon vanilla extract

1/4 teaspoon salt

✳ Cover the dried figs with boiling water and set aside until soft, about 2 hours. Drain the figs, cut into quarters and place in a food processor. Add the eggs and process until smooth, about 1 minute.

✳ Combine the milk and sugar in a medium saucepan and place over low heat. Stir until the sugar dissolves and the milk comes to a boil. Immediately remove from the heat. With the food processor running, slowly pour the hot milk into the fig mixture through the feed tube. Process until completely smooth. Pour the mixture into a large, clean bowl and let cool slightly. Stir in the cream, vanilla and salt. Cover and refrigerate until cold, or overnight.

✳ Stir the chilled custard, then freeze in 1 or 2 batches in your ice cream machine according to the manufacturer's instructions. When finished, the ice cream will be soft, but ready to eat. For firmer ice cream, transfer it to a freezer-safe container and freeze for at least 2 hours.

SERVES 4 TO 6

THIS IS A good WAY TO USE BANANAS THAT ARE GETTING TOO ripe. ITS ONLY DRAWBACK IS ALSO ONE OF ITS ASSETS—IT MUST BE made IN ADVANCE.

MAKES ABOUT 1 QUART

DRIED FIGS HAVE A MORE intense FLAVOR THAN FRESH FIGS, MAKING THEM perfect FOR ICE CREAM. LOOK FOR ones THAT ARE SEMIMOIST, NOT HARD OR DESICCATED.

Variations

Fig-Almond Ice Cream

✳ Add ¼ teaspoon almond extract along with the vanilla extract. Add ½ cup chopped toasted almonds to the machine when the ice cream is semifrozen. Allow the machine to mix in the nuts. Proceed with the recipe as directed.

Fig Tart Ice Cream

✳ Substitute honey for sugar. Add 1 teaspoon grated fresh orange zest and 3 crumbled graham crackers to the machine when the ice cream is semifrozen. Allow the machine to mix in the additional ingredients. Proceed with the recipe as directed.

Spiced Figgie Pudding Ice Cream

✳ Add ½ teaspoon ground cinnamon, ¼ teaspoon ground nutmeg and ⅛ teaspoon ground mace to the milk along with the sugar. Proceed with the recipe as directed.

Fig-Cookie Ice Cream

✳ Add ½ cup crumbled sugar cookies to the machine when the ice cream is semifrozen. Allow the machine to mix in the cookies. Proceed with the recipe as directed.

Promised Land Ice Cream

✳ Add ¼ cup chopped dried dates, ¼ cup raisins and ½ cup crumbled mandelbrot or other dry cake to the machine when the ice cream is semifrozen. Allow the machine to mix in the additional ingredients. Proceed with the recipe as directed.

Chocolate Malt Ice Cream

BRUCE WEINSTEIN/REPRINTED FROM *THE ULTIMATE ICE CREAM BOOK* **(WILLIAM MORROW)**

3 ounces unsweetened baking chocolate,
    chopped
1 cup sugar
4 to 6 tablespoons malted milk powder

2 cups half-and-half
2 large eggs, lightly beaten
1 cup heavy cream
2 teaspoons vanilla extract

✻ Combine the chopped chocolate, sugar, malted milk powder and half-and-half in a heavy medium saucepan. Place over low heat and stir until the chocolate is completely melted and the sugar is dissolved. Bring the mixture to a simmer and cook for 1 minute, stirring constantly. Slowly beat the hot half-and-half mixture into the eggs in a bowl. Return the entire mixture back to the pan and place over low heat. Stir constantly with a whisk or wooden spoon until the custard thickens slightly. Be careful not to let the mixture boil or the eggs will scramble. Remove from the heat and pour the hot chocolate custard through a strainer into a large, clean bowl.

✻ At this point the custard should be homogenous. If you see specks of chocolate, allow the custard to cool slightly, then pour the custard into a blender and blend for 30 seconds. Pour back into the bowl. Stir in the cream and vanilla. Cover and refrigerate until cold, or up to overnight.

✻ Stir the chilled custard, then freeze in 1 or 2 batches in your ice cream machine according to the manufacturer's instructions. When finished, the ice cream will be soft, but ready to eat. For firmer ice cream, transfer to a freezer-safe container and freeze for at least 2 hours.

Variations

Chocolate-Banana Malt Ice Cream

✱ Slice 2 small bananas thinly. Toss with 2 tablespoons sugar and 2 tablespoons brandy or banana liqueur. Let the fruit macerate for at least 2 hours. Add this mixture to the custard before freezing. Proceed with the recipe as directed.

Texas Chocolate Malt Ice Cream

✱ Add ½ teaspoon ground cinnamon to the custard along with the malted milk powder. Proceed with the recipe as directed, adding ½ cup chopped toasted pecans to the machine when the ice cream is semifrozen. Allow the machine to mix in the nuts. Proceed with the recipe as directed.

Chocolate-Peanut Butter Malt Ice Cream

✱ Beat ¼ cup smooth peanut butter into the hot custard before straining. Proceed with the recipe as directed, adding ½ cup chopped peanut butter cup candies to the machine when the ice cream is semifrozen. Allow the machine to mix in the candy. Proceed with the recipe as directed.

Chocolate Fudge Malt Ice Cream

✱ Add ½ cup chopped chocolate fudge (with or without nuts) to the machine when the ice cream is semifrozen. Allow the machine to mix in the candy. Proceed with the recipe as directed.

Chocolate Malted Ball Ice Cream

✱ Add ½ cup chopped malted milk balls to the machine when the ice cream is semifrozen. Allow the machine to mix in the candy. Proceed with the recipe as directed.

Candy Cane Ice Cream Torte

MARLENE SOROSKY

½ gallon good-quality chocolate ice cream
1 quart good-quality pink peppermint ice
   cream

About forty 3-inch candy canes
One 4.5-ounce package red fruit leather,
   such as Fruit by the Foot

✳ Spoon the chocolate ice cream around the sides of an 8-inch springform pan, forming a 2- to 2½-inch border (you will not use all of the ice cream). Spoon the peppermint ice cream into the center. Smooth the top and freeze until firm.

✳ Remove the sides of the springform. Arrange the candy canes facing the same direction around the chocolate ice cream to resemble a picket fence. Coarsely chop the remaining candy canes and sprinkle over the peppermint ice cream. At this point the torte can be frozen overnight.

✳ Up to 1 hour before serving, tie a "ribbon" of fruit leather around the candy canes. Make a "bow" of the fruit leather and place on the ribbon. Freeze until ready to serve.

Buttermilk Pie

JOYCE WHITE/REPRINTED FROM *SOUL FOOD* (HARPERCOLLINS)

One 9-inch pie crust, baked
Beaten egg white
$2/3$ cup sugar
3 tablespoons flour
1 cup buttermilk
2 eggs, beaten

4 tablespoons ($1/2$ stick) butter or
    margarine, melted
$1/2$ teaspoon vanilla extract
$1/2$ teaspoon lemon extract
$1/2$ cup grated or shredded coconut

✳ Preheat the oven to 425°F.

✳ Prick the pie crust all over and brush lightly with beaten egg white. Set on the lower shelf of the hot oven and bake for 5 minutes. Remove from the oven, cool on a wire rack.

✳ In a large bowl, combine the sugar, flour and $1/2$ cup of the buttermilk. Mix well. Add the eggs, remaining $1/2$ cup of the buttermilk, butter or margarine, and the vanilla and lemon extracts to the bowl. Mix until well blended.

✳ Pour the filling into the cooled pie shell. Sprinkle the top with the coconut. Set the pan in the hot oven on the middle shelf.

✳ Bake the pie at 425°F for 10 minutes, then reduce the oven heat to 350°F. Bake for 30 to 35 minutes, or until the pie filling is fluffy and a knife inserted into the center comes out clean. Cool on a wire rack. Cut into wedges to serve.

MAKES ONE 9-INCH
PIE; SERVES 6

BUTTERMILK'S LIGHT, tangy FLAVOR COMBINES WITH nutty SHREDDED COCONUT FOR AN INTERESTING PIE FILLING. IT'S AN easy RECIPE TO PUT TOGETHER, TOO, SUITABLE FOR ANY night OF THE WEEK.

Cranberry Window Pie

ROSE LEVY BERANBAUM/REPRINTED FROM *THE PIE AND PASTRY BIBLE* **(SCRIBNER)**

Basic Flaky Pie Crust (*recipe follows*)

Filling
One 12-ounce package fresh or frozen
  cranberries (about 3 1/2 cups), rinsed,
  picked over and dried

1 1/4 cups plus 1 tablespoon sugar
1 tablespoon freshly grated orange zest
3 tablespoons Lyle's Golden Syrup, or light
  corn syrup
1 tablespoon milk
2 tablespoons freshly squeezed orange juice

✱ Remove the dough for the bottom crust from the refrigerator. If necessary, let it stand for about 10 minutes, or until it is soft enough to roll.

✱ On a floured pastry cloth or between two sheets of lightly floured plastic wrap, roll the bottom crust ⅛-inch thick or less, and large enough to cut a 12-inch circle. Transfer it to the pie pan. Trim the edge almost even with the edge of the pan. Cover it with plastic wrap and refrigerate for a minimum of 30 minutes and a maximum of 3 hours.

✱ Cut each cranberry in half and place in a medium bowl. Mix the cut cranberries with ¾ cup of the sugar, orange zest and 1 tablespoon of the syrup. Pour the mixture into the pie shell.

✱ Roll out the top crust large enough to cut a 12-inch circle. Use an expandable flan ring or a cardboard template and a sharp knife as a guide to cut out the circle.

✱ Moisten the edges of the bottom crust with water and place the top crust over the fruit. Tuck the overhang under the bottom crust border and press down all around the top to seal it. Crimp the border using a fork or your fingers. With a sharp knife, cut a 3-inch-long plus sign in the center of the crust and pull back the pieces of dough to form a window. Cover the pie loosely with plastic wrap and refrigerate for 1 hour before baking to chill and relax the pastry. (This will maintain flakiness and help to keep the crust from shrinking.)

✱ Preheat the oven to 425°F at least 20 minutes before baking. Set an oven rack at the lowest level and place a baking stone or baking sheet on it before preheating. Place a Teflon-type liner or a large piece of greased foil on top to catch any juices.

✱ Brush the crust with the milk and sprinkle with 1 tablespoon of the sugar. (For a very even coating of sugar, place the sugar in a strainer and tap the rim of the strainer.)

✱ Set the pie directly on the foil-topped baking stone and bake for 10 minutes. Reduce the oven heat to 375°F and continue baking for 30 minutes.

(continued on next page)

✳ Meanwhile, in a small saucepan or a microwave, combine the remaining ½ cup sugar, 2 tablespoons syrup, and the orange juice. Bring to a boil, stirring constantly, and simmer over low heat for 2 minutes, until the liquid is reduced to ½ cup.

✳ Pour the liquid into the center of the pie. Reduce the oven heat to 325°F and continue baking for 10 to 20 minutes, or until the center bubbles.

✳ Cool the pie on a rack for at least 3 hours before serving. Store at room temperature for up to 2 days.

Basic Flaky Pie Crust

14 tablespoons (1³/₄ sticks) unsalted
    butter, cold
2¹/₄ cups plus 2 tablespoons pastry flour
    or bleached all-purpose flour
¹/₄ plus ¹/₈ teaspoon salt

¹/₄ teaspoon baking powder, optional
    (if not using, double the salt)
5 to 7 tablespoons ice water
1 tablespoon cider vinegar

✳ Divide the butter into two parts, 9 tablespoons and 5 tablespoons. Cut each portion of butter into ¾-inch cubes and wrap each portion with plastic wrap. Refrigerate the larger amount and freeze the smaller for at least 30 minutes. Place the flour, salt and optional baking powder in a locking gallon-size freezer bag and freeze for at least 30 minutes.

✳ Place the flour mixture in a food processor with the metal blade and process for a few seconds to combine. Set the bag aside. Add the larger amount of butter cubes to the flour and process for about 20 seconds, or until the mixture resembles coarse meal. Add the remaining frozen butter cubes and pulse until all of the frozen butter is the size of peas.

✳ Add the lowest amount of the ice water and the vinegar and pulse 6 times. Pinch a small amount of the mixture together between your fingers. If it does not hold together, add ½ of the remaining water and pulse 3 times. Try pinching the mixture again. If necessary, add the remaining water, pulsing 3 times to incorporate it. The mixture will be in particles and will not hold together without being pinched. Spoon the mixture into the plastic bag. (For a double-crust pie, it is easiest to divide the mixture in half at this point.)

✳ Holding both ends of the bag opening with your fingers, knead the mixture by alternately pressing it, from the outside of the bag, with the knuckles and heels of your hands until the mixture holds together in one piece and feels slightly stretchy when pulled.

✳ Wrap the dough with plastic wrap, flatten it into a disc (or discs) and refrigerate for at least 45 minutes, preferably overnight. *Makes one 9-inch double-crust pie.*

Crustless Apple Crumb Pie

ROSE LEVY BERANBAUM/REPRINTED FROM *THE PIE AND PASTRY BIBLE* **(SCRIBNER)**

1½ pounds baking apples (about 3 large), peeled, cored and sliced ½-inch thick
1½ teaspoons freshly squeezed lemon juice
2 tablespoons packed light brown sugar
2 tablespoons granulated sugar
¾ teaspoon ground cinnamon
⅛ teaspoon freshly grated nutmeg
⅛ teaspoon salt
1 tablespoon unsalted butter

Topping
2 tablespoons plus 2 teaspoons packed light brown sugar
1 tablespoon granulated sugar
½ cup walnut halves
1/16 teaspoon salt
¾ teaspoon ground cinnamon
½ cup bleached all-purpose flour
¼ cup (½ stick) unsalted butter, slightly softened
¾ teaspoon pure vanilla extract

✳ Preheat the oven to 400°F at least 20 minutes before baking time. Set an oven rack on the second level from the bottom. Set a greased foil-lined baking sheet under the pie to catch the juices.

✳ In a large bowl, combine the apples, lemon juice, sugars, cinnamon, nutmeg and salt and toss to mix. Let the mixture stand for 30 minutes to 1 hour.

✳ To make the topping, pulse together the sugars, nuts, salt and cinnamon in a food processor until the nuts are coarsely chopped. Add the flour, butter and vanilla and pulse until the mixture is coarse and crumbly, about 20 times. Empty it into a small bowl and with your fingertips, lightly pinch together the mixture to form little clumps.

✳ Transfer the apples and their juices to a colander suspended over a bowl to capture the liquid. The mixture will exude about ¼ cup of liquid. In a small saucepan (preferably with a nonstick surface), reduce this liquid, over medium-high heat, with the butter, to 2 tablespoons. Pour the hot liquid over the apples in a bowl, tossing them gently.

✳ Transfer the apples with the juices to a 9-inch pie pan. Cover the dish with foil and make a 1-inch slash in the middle. Bake the apples for 30 minutes.

✳ Remove the foil and sprinkle the surface evenly with the topping. Bake for 20 to 25 minutes, or until the topping is crisp and golden brown, the fruit juices are bubbling thickly around the edges, and the apples feel tender but not mushy when a small sharp knife is inserted. Cool on a rack.

✳ Serve the crumb pie warm or at room temperature. Store at room temperature for up to 2 days; refrigerated, up to 3 days.

NOTE: If a deeper filling is desired, you can increase the filling by 1½ times and the initial baking time to 40 minutes.

SERVES 6

THIS pie IS FOR THOSE WHO EAT THEIR APPLES IN THE FORM OF A crisp, WHICH IS A CRUSTLESS PIE WITH A crumb TOPPING. SERVE THIS PIE warm, ACCOMPANIED BY CARAMEL OR VANILLA ICE CREAM

Chocolate Peanut Butter Mousse Tart

ROSE LEVY BERANBAUM/REPRINTED FROM *THE PIE AND PASTRY BIBLE* (SCRIBNER)

Peanut Butter Mousse

7 tablespoons cream cheese, softened
1/2 cup peanut butter, preferably Jif, at
    room temperature
1/4 cup sugar
1 teaspoon vanilla extract
3/4 cup heavy cream, softly whipped

Sweet Peanut Butter Cookie Tart Crust
    (see page 154)

Milk Chocolate Ganache

One 3-ounce bar milk chocolate
2/3 of a 3-ounce bar bittersweet chocolate
1/3 cup heavy cream
1/8 teaspoon vanilla extract

✱ To make the peanut butter mousse, beat the cream cheese, peanut butter and sugar in a mixer bowl, preferably with the whisk beater, until uniform in color. On low speed, beat in the vanilla. Beat in 1/4 cup of the whipped cream until just incorporated. With a large rubber spatula, fold in the rest of the whipped cream until blended but still airy. Scrape the mousse into the prepared tart crust and smooth the surface so that it is level. Refrigerate the tart while preparing the ganache.

✱ To make the ganache, break the chocolates into several pieces into the bowl of a food processor. Process until the chocolate is very finely ground.

✱ In a heatproof glass measuring cup, if using a microwave oven, or in a small saucepan, bring the cream to a boil. With the food processor running, immediately pour it through the feed tube onto the chocolate. Process until smooth, about 15 seconds, scraping the sides of the bowl once or twice. Add the vanilla and pulse a few times to incorporate it. Pour the ganache into a liquid measuring cup or bowl. Let cool to room temperature.

✱ Pour the ganache over the peanut butter mousse in a circular motion, so that it does not land too heavily in any one spot and cause a depression. With a small metal spatula, start by spreading the ganache to the edges of the pastry, then spread it evenly to cover the entire surface. Make a spiral pattern by lightly pressing the spatula against the surface and running it from the outside to the center. Refrigerate the tart for at least 2 hours to set.

✱ Remove the tart from the refrigerator at least 15 minutes before serving. Unmold the tart and cut with a sharp thin blade, dipped in hot water between each slice. Serve lightly chilled or at room temperature.

SERVES 6 TO 8

AN easy PEANUT BUTTER MOUSSE AND MILK CHOCOLATE FILLING top A SWEET PEANUT BUTTER cookie CRUST. THOUGH THE INGREDIENTS ARE FAMILIAR, THE PIE MAKES AN elegant SPECIAL OCCASION TREAT.

Sweet Peanut Butter Cookie Tart Crust

ROSE LEVY BERANBAUM/REPRINTED FROM *THE PIE AND PASTRY BIBLE* (SCRIBNER)

MAKES ONE 9¹/₂-
TO 10-INCH CRUST

IF YOU love PEANUT

BUTTER cookies, THIS

IS YOUR CRUST. IT IS ACTU-

ALLY Rose's PEANUT

BUTTER COOKIE BAKED

IN A TART PAN.

¹/₂ cup bleached all-purpose flour
¹/₂ teaspoon baking soda
¹/₁₆ teaspoon salt
¹/₄ cup packed light brown sugar
2 tablespoons granulated sugar,
   preferably superfine

4 tablespoons (¹/₂ stick) unsalted butter,
   softened if using a mixer, or cold, cut into
   1-inch cubes if using a food processor
¹/₂ cup smooth peanut butter, preferably
   Jif, at room temperature
¹/₂ large egg (beat before measuring)
¹/₄ teaspoon vanilla extract

✱ **Electric Mixer Method:** Into a small bowl, sift together the flour, baking soda and salt. Whisk to combine well. In a mixing bowl, beat the sugars until well mixed. Add the softened butter and peanut butter and beat for several minutes, or until very smooth and creamy. Add the egg and vanilla extract and beat until incorporated, scraping the sides of the bowl. At low speed, gradually beat in the flour mixture until just incorporated.

✱ **Food Processor Method:** Into a small bowl, sift together the flour, baking soda and salt, then whisk to combine well. In a food processor, process the sugars for several minutes or until very fine. With the motor running, add the cold butter cubes. Add the peanut butter and process until smooth and creamy, about 10 seconds. With the motor running, add the egg and vanilla extract and process until incorporated. Scrape the sides of the bowl. Add the flour mixture and pulse just until incorporated.

✱ **For both methods:** Scrape the dough into a bowl and refrigerate for at least 1 hour, or overnight.

✱ Press the dough evenly into a 9¹/₂-inch fluted tart pan with a removable bottom. Cover it with plastic wrap and refrigerate for at least 1 hour. (You will probably have about 2 tablespoons of excess dough, which can be baked as cookies.)

✱ Preheat the oven to 375°F. Bake the tart shell, without weights, for 10 to 12 minutes, or until golden. It will puff at first and then settle down toward the end of baking. The sides will be soft but spring back when touched gently with a finger. Cool the tart crust on a wire rack.

Supernatural Brownies

NICK MALGIERI/REPRINTED FROM *CHOCOLATE* (HARPERCOLLINS)

16 tablespoons (2 sticks) unsalted butter
8 ounces bittersweet or semisweet choco-
    late, cut into ¹/₄-inch pieces
4 large eggs
¹/₂ teaspoon salt
1 cup granulated sugar

1 cup firmly packed dark brown sugar
2 teaspoons vanilla extract
1 cup all-purpose flour
Ice cream (optional)
Nick Malgieri's Hot Fudge Sauce, page 164
    (optional)

✱ Set a rack at the middle level of the oven and preheat to 350°F. Butter a 13-by-9-by-2-inch pan and line with buttered parchment or foil.

✱ Bring a saucepan of water to a boil and turn off the heat. Combine the butter and chocolate in a heatproof bowl and set it over the pan of water. Stir occasionally until the mixture is melted.

✱ Whisk the eggs together in a large bowl, then whisk in the salt, sugars and vanilla. Stir in the chocolate-butter mixture, then fold in the flour.

✱ Pour the batter into the prepared pan and spread evenly. Bake for about 45 minutes, until the top has formed a shiny crust and the batter is moderately firm. Cool in the pan on a rack. Wrap the pan with plastic wrap and keep it at room temperature or refrigerated until the next day.

✱ To cut the brownies, unmold them onto a cutting board, remove the paper, and replace with another cutting board. Turn the cake right-side up and trim away the edges. Cut the brownies into 2-inch squares.

✱ Serve the brownies on their own, or with ice cream and hot fudge sauce as a scrumptious brownie sundae.

NOTE: The best way to store the brownies is to wrap them individually and keep them at room temperature in a tin or plastic container with a tight-fitting cover. Or freeze them.

VARIATION: Add 2 cups (½ pound) walnut or pecan pieces to the batter.

MAKES ABOUT 24 2-INCH-SQUARE BROWNIES

THOUGH THE name SOUNDS AN EXAGGERATION, YOU'LL agree THAT THESE BROWNIES ARE OUT OF THIS WORLD. TRY THEM IN A BOWL ACCOMPANIED BY ICE CREAM AND NICK'S hot FUDGE SAUCE FOR AN otherworldy EXPERIENCE.

Chocolate "Rocks"

GERALD HIRIGOYEN/REPRINTED FROM *THE BASQUE KITCHEN* **(HARPERCOLLINS)**

MAKES 12 ROCKS

THE SHAPE OF THESE

DESSERTS REMINDS GERALD

OF THE craggy ROCKS

JUST OFF THE COAST OF

BIARRITZ. Chocolate

MERINGUES ARE MOUNDED

WITH CHOCOLATE MOUSSE

AND flecked WITH

COCOA, JUST AS THE ROCKS

THERE ARE FLECKED WITH

sea FOAM.

Meringues
Melted unsalted butter for brushing
 the pan
3 egg whites
$2/3$ cup sugar
1 tablespoon unsweetened cocoa powder

Mousse
4 egg yolks
$1/4$ cup plus 2 tablespoons sugar
5 ounces good-quality European semisweet or bittersweet chocolate
$1 1/4$ cups ($2 1/2$ sticks) unsalted butter, cut
 into cubes

Confectioners' sugar or unsweetened
 cocoa powder for dusting (optional)

✳ Preheat the oven to 275°F. Line a large baking sheet with parchment paper and brush it with melted butter; set aside.

✳ To make the meringues, place the egg whites in the workbowl of a standing mixer fitted with a whisk attachment. Beat the egg whites to the hard-peak stage while slowly adding ⅓ cup of the sugar.

✳ Combine the remaining ⅓ cup sugar and the cocoa powder, then fold into the egg whites. Spoon the meringue into 12 individual mounds on the baking sheet.

✳ Bake the meringues until they are crisp, approximately 1 hour. Set them aside on a rack to cool for at least 30 minutes.

✳ To make the mousse, beat the egg yolks and ¼ cup sugar in a standing mixer fitted with the whisk attachment until frothy and pale yellow in color.

✳ Melt the chocolate and butter together in a heatproof bowl set over a pan of gently simmering water, whisking until smooth and creamy. Remove the bowl from the heat, and immediately stir the egg yolk mixture into the chocolate; set aside.

✳ Whip the egg whites to the hard-peak stage, while adding the remaining 2 tablespoons sugar. Gently fold them into the chocolate batter, using a large spatula, just until evenly combined. Place the mousse in the refrigerator until it firms slightly, about 30 minutes.

✳ Carefully shape 2 to 3 rounded tablespoonfuls of the mousse on top of each of the meringues. If desired, dust the chocolate "rocks" with confectioners' sugar and/or cocoa powder. Serve chilled or at room temperature.

MAKES 36 TO
40 COOKIES

THE BASE OF THE
turtle IS BROWN SUGAR
COOKIE DOUGH, WHICH
IS PLACED UPON "LEGS" OF
pecan HALVES. IT'S
BAKED, TOPPED WITH
marshmallows, AND
RETURNED TO THE OVEN
JUST LONG ENOUGH
FOR THE MARSHMALLOWS
TO SLIGHTLY melt. THE
MARSHMALLOW TOP IS
coated WITH DARK
CHOCOLATE AND YOU'VE
GOT A deliciously
EDIBLE TURTLE.

Marshmallow Turtle Cookies

MARLENE SOROSKY / REPRINTED FROM *SEASON'S GREETINGS* (CHRONICLE)

One 10-ounce package pecan halves (about 2 1/2 cups)
Brown Sugar Cookie Dough (*recipe follows*)

20 marshmallows, cut in half horizontally
6 ounces semisweet chocolate, chopped

✳ Preheat the oven to 325°F.

✳ Place 4 pecan halves in clusters on parchment-lined or greased baking sheets. Break off small pieces of dough and roll into 1-inch balls. Place a ball in the center of each of the 4 pecans. Lightly press the dough into the pecans.

✳ Bake the cookies for 10 to 15 minutes, or until the bottoms are lightly browned. Remove the cookies from the oven and top each with a marshmallow half, cut-side down. Return to the oven for 1 minute. Immediately press the marshmallow down lightly. Transfer to racks to cool.

✳ Melt the chocolate in the top of a double boiler. Dip the cookies into the chocolate to cover the marshmallow. Cool until the chocolate has hardened.

✳ The cookies can be refrigerated or stored in an airtight container in a cool place for several weeks. They can also be frozen; thaw in a single layer.

Brown Sugar Cookie Dough

10 tablespoons (1 1/4 sticks) butter or margarine
2/3 cup firmly packed light or golden brown sugar
1 egg

1 teaspoon vanilla extract
1/4 teaspoon salt
1 3/4 cups all-purpose flour
1/2 teaspoon baking powder
1/2 teaspoon baking soda

✳ In a mixing bowl with an electric mixer, beat the butter and sugar until light and fluffy. Beat in the egg and vanilla. Add the salt, flour, baking powder and baking soda, mixing until blended.

Snickerdoodles

REPRINTED FROM *A KLUTZ GUIDE: CLASSIC COOKIES* **(KLUTZ)**

$^1/_2$ cup (1 stick) butter
$^3/_4$ cup sugar
1 egg
1 teaspoon vanilla extract
$1^1/_3$ cups flour
1 teaspoon baking soda
Pinch of salt

Topping
$^1/_4$ cup sugar
1 tablespoon ground cinnamon

✻ Preheat the oven to 350°F.

✻ In a bowl, beat the butter and sugar together until light and fluffy. Add the egg and vanilla and beat until smooth. Add the flour, baking soda and salt and mix again.

✻ Mix the topping ingredients in a shallow bowl or flat pan.

✻ Use your hands to form the dough into walnut-sized balls and roll in the topping. Place the balls on a baking sheet. Press down with the bottom of a glass or a wooden spoon.

✻ Bake for 10 minutes. Cool on a rack.

MAKES 24 COOKIES

A GOOD RECIPE FOR THE kids TO MAKE, THESE cinnamonny treats ARE GREAT FOR BOTH BROWN BAGGING AND AFTER-SCHOOL SNACKING.

Mega Ultra Incredicookies

REPRINTED FROM *A KLUTZ GUIDE: CLASSIC COOKIES* (KLUTZ)

$1/2$ cup (1 stick) butter, softened
$1/4$ cup vegetable oil
$1/2$ cup peanut butter
$3/4$ cup granulated sugar
$3/4$ cup brown sugar
2 eggs
1 teaspoon vanilla extract

$1^1/2$ teaspoons baking soda
$1/2$ teaspoon salt
1 cup flour
2 cups rolled oats (not instant)

Goodies
$1^1/2$ cups chocolate chips, or M&Ms, or
trail mix, or a combination

✳ Preheat the oven to 375°F.

✳ With a mixer, beat the butter, oil, peanut butter, sugars, eggs and vanilla until smooth.

✳ Stop the mixer and scrape down the bowl and beaters. Add in everything else (choose one of the goodies) and mix again.

✳ Use an ice cream scoop or big spoon to make 4 cookies at a time on an ungreased baking sheet.

✳ Bake the cookies for 12 to 14 minutes. Cool for 1 minute on the baking sheet, then on a rack.

Wreath Cookies

MARLENE SOROSKY/REPRINTED FROM *SEASON'S GREETINGS* (CHRONICLE)

Brown Sugar Cookie Dough (see page 158)
6 ounces semisweet chocolate, melted
   (optional)
Confectioners' sugar (optional)

Milk (optional)
Pecan halves, silver ball decorations, sliced
   almonds, and/or glacéed cherries

MAKES 3 WREATHS

THESE WREATHS ARE MADE BY joining 12 COOKIES TOGETHER IN A CIRCLE. WHEN THEY BAKE, THEY SPREAD INTO A lovely ROUND AND FLUTED WREATH. CUT CARDBOARD ROUNDS A LITTLE SMALLER THAN THE WREATHS AND COVER THEM WITH ATTRACTIVE doilies. THEN YOU CAN EASILY STORE THE wreaths IN THE FREEZER, READY TO PULL OUT AT A MOMENT'S NOTICE.

✴ Preheat the oven to 325°F. Line baking sheets with parchment paper or grease them.

✴ Divide the dough into 3 equal parts. Working with ⅓ of the dough at a time, break off 12 pieces of dough and roll them into twelve 1-inch balls. Place the balls ½-inch apart on the baking sheet, forming a 6-inch circle. Flatten the balls slightly. Repeat the process with the remaining ⅔ of the dough, making 2 more circles.

✴ Bake the cookie circles for 15 minutes, or until the bottoms are lightly browned. If baking 2 sheets of cookies at a time, rotate their positions halfway through the baking time. Cool the cookies for 15 minutes and remove them from the baking sheet. Do not be concerned if they break.

✴ The wreaths can be frosted with melted chocolate or confectioners' sugar mixed with just enough milk to make a spreading consistency. Before the frosting sets, decorate the wreathes with nuts, silver balls, and/or glacéed cherries.

✴ The wreaths can be stored airtight for several weeks in a cool place. They can also be frozen; thaw in a single layer.

NOTE: To tie a bow through the top, make 2 holes using the handle of a wooden spoon in the center of two of the balls of dough. Bake for 10 minutes; press the holes again. When cool, tie colored ribbon through the holes.

Popcorn Trees

MARLENE SOROSKY/REPRINTED FROM *SEASON'S GREETINGS* **(CHRONICLE)**

2¹/₂ cups confectioners' sugar
1 egg white
1¹/₂ tablespoons water
6 drops green food coloring

6 sugar cones
3 cups popped corn
Red cinnamon candies

✱ Stir the confectioners' sugar, unbeaten egg white and water together to make a frosting. Add the food coloring and stir to blend. Spread the frosting over the outside of the cones, using about 2 tablespoons per cone to cover them completely.

✱ While the icing is still soft, press popped corn all over the surface of the cones. Dot with the cinnamon candies to resemble Christmas tree decorations.

MAKES 6 TREES

KEEP THESE whimsical RED AND GREEN POPCORN trees AROUND WHEN THE YOUNG ONES COME BY FOR A holiday CELEBRATION.

Applesauce-Cinnamon Cut-Out Decorations

MARLENE SOROSKY/REPRINTED FROM *SEASON'S GREETINGS* **(CHRONICLE)**

¹/₂ cup smooth applesauce
¹/₂ cup plus 2 tablespoons ground cinnamon, plus more for rolling

Scraps of material, buttons, glitter candies, etc., for decorating

✱ Preheat the oven to 250°F.

✱ In a medium bowl, stir together the applesauce and ¹/₂ cup of the cinnamon. Add the remaining 2 tablespoons cinnamon and work with your hands to form the mixture into a dough. If it is sticky, work in more cinnamon a little at a time.

✱ Sprinkle a work surface with cinnamon. Roll the dough ¹/₄-inch thick. Using cookie cutters, cut the dough into the desired shapes. Place the shapes on a baking sheet and bake until dry, 50 to 60 minutes. Cool and decorate as desired.

MAKES ABOUT NINE 3-INCH CUT-OUTS

ALTHOUGH THEY PROBABLY WON'T make YOU SICK IF YOU EAT THESE, THEY SURE DON'T TASTE VERY good. BUT THEY DEFINITELY MAKE TERRIFIC decorations.

Strawberry Malt

BRUCE WEINSTEIN/REPRINTED FROM *THE ULTIMATE ICE CREAM BOOK* **(WILLIAM MORROW)**

**MAKES ONE
16-OUNCE DRINK**

FRESH OR frozen
STRAWBERRIES WILL WORK
HERE. IN FACT, IF YOU USE
fresh BERRIES, YOU
SHOULD PARTIALLY FREEZE
THEM BEFORE BLENDING.
IF YOU USE FROZEN BERRIES,
THAW THEM PARTIALLY
BEFORE blending.

12 large strawberries, partially frozen
2 scoops strawberry ice cream
3 heaping tablespoons malted milk powder
1 cup milk

2 tablespoons strawberry topping or strawberry preserves

✳ Place all of the ingredients in a blender. Pulse the blender on and off until the mixture blends easily. Blend on high speed for 30 seconds or until smooth.

Variations

Strawberry Coconut Malt

✳ Substitute unsweetened coconut milk for the dairy milk.

Strawberry Shake

✳ If you prefer a plain strawberry shake, simply omit the malted milk powder.

Nick Malgieri's Hot Fudge Sauce

NICK MALGIERI/REPRINTED FROM *CHOCOLATE* **(HARPERCOLLINS)**

MAKES ABOUT 2 CUPS

THIS IS ONE OF THOSE
REALLY rich HOT FUDGE
SAUCES THAT HARDENS
AS IT HITS ICE CREAM.
IT'S great TO USE
AS THE sauce FOR A
BROWNIE SUNDAE.

1/4 cup water
1 cup light corn syrup
1 1/3 cups sugar
1/4 teaspoon salt
4 ounces unsweetened chocolate, coarsely
chopped

1/2 cup unsweetened Dutch processed
cocoa powder
4 tablespoons (1/2 stick) unsalted butter
1/4 cup heavy cream
1 tablespoon vanilla extract

✳ Combine the water, corn syrup and sugar in a nonreactive pan and bring it to a boil, stirring often, until all of the sugar crystals have melted. Boil for 1 minute without stirring.

✳ Remove from the heat and add the salt and the chocolate. Let stand for 2 minutes, until the chocolate has melted, then whisk until smooth.

✳ Sift the cocoa into a mixing bowl and stir in enough of the liquid mixture to make a paste, then stir the cocoa paste smoothly back into the syrup.
Whisk in the remaining ingredients.

✳ Store the sauce in a tightly covered jar in the refrigerator. Reheat the opened jar over simmering water before serving.

Bruce Weinstein's Hot Fudge Sauce

BRUCE WEINSTEIN/REPRINTED FROM *THE ULTIMATE ICE CREAM BOOK* **(WILLIAM MORROW)**

4 ounces bittersweet or semisweet
  chocolate, chopped
2 ounces unsweetened chocolate, chopped
3 tablespoons unsalted butter

1/3 cup heavy cream
1/3 cup sugar
1/3 cup light corn syrup
1 teaspoon vanilla extract

* Melt the bittersweet and unsweetened chocolates with the butter in a double boiler or in a large metal bowl set over a pan of simmering water.

* Meanwhile, warm the cream in a medium saucepan over low heat. Add the sugar and corn syrup to the cream and stir until the sugar dissolves completely. Add the warm sweetened cream to the melted chocolate. Continue to heat the mixture over simmering water for 10 minutes, stirring constantly. Stir in the vanilla. Serve hot.

Variations

Cherry Fudge Sauce

* Pour 2 tablespoons cherry brandy over 1/4 cup dried cherries and set aside for 1 hour before preparing the sauce. Add the cherries and liqueur along with the vanilla.

Southern Fudge Sauce

* Add 1/2 cup chopped toasted pecans along with the vanilla.

Marshmallow Fudge Meltdown

* Add 1 cup miniature marshmallows and 1/2 cup chopped toasted hazelnuts along with the vanilla. Stir until the marshmallows melt completely.

Tropical Fudge Sauce

* Add 1/2 cup toasted sweetened coconut along with the vanilla. Optional: add 2 tablespoons coconut-flavored rum.

MAKE ABOUT 2 CUPS

THIS topping IS PERHAPS THE CLASSIC OF ALL classics. VARY IT TO SUIT THE occasion, OR YOUR MOOD.

INDEX

PERMISSIONS

From *The Barbecue! Bible* by Steven Raichlen (Workman Publishing, 1998) © 1998 by Steven Raichlen: Basic Chimichurri, Catalan Tomato Bread, Grilled Corn with Shadon Beni Butter, Grilled Dilled Tomatoes, Grilled Gazpacho, Grilled Pita Chips, Grilled Plantains, Grilled Sugar-Dipped Pineapple, Middle Eastern Eggplant Puree with Tahini, Montevidean Stuffed Beef Roll, Piri-Piri Chicken, The Pompano Grille's Fire-Grilled Banana Split

From *The Basque Kitchen: Tempting Food from the Pyrenees* by Gerald Hirigoyen with Cameron Hirigoyen (HarperCollins Publishers, 1999) © 1999 by Gerald Hirigoyen and Cameron Hirigoyen: Chocolate "Rocks," Fava Bean Gratin, Lamb Stew with Mixed Nut Pesto, Peppers Stuffed with Salt Cod

From *Biker Billy's Freeway-A-Fire* by Bill Hufnagle (William Morrow, 2000) © 2000 by Bill Hufnagle: Chipotle Cheese Soup, Hot Chili Pie, Peaches in Paradise

From *The Cake Bible* by Rose Levy Beranbaum (William Morrow, 1988) © 1988 by Rose Levy Beranbaum: Chocolate Domingo Cake, Perfect Pound Cake

From *The Chinese Kitchen* by Eileen Yin-Fei Lo (William Morrow, 1999) © 1999 by Eileen Yin-Fei Lo: Harmonious Vegetable Stir-Fry, Longevity Noodles, Pepper Steak, Steamed Lemon Chicken

From *Chocolate: From Simple Cookies to Extravagant Showstoppers* by Nick Malgieri (Harper Collins Publishers, 1998) © 1998 by Nick Malgieri: Hot Fudge Sauce, Lemon-Scented White Cake with Milk Chocolate Frosting, Supernatural Brownies

From *Cocktail Food: 50 Finger Foods with Attitude* by Mary Corpening Barber and Sara Corpening Whiteford with Lori Lyn Narlock (Chronicle Books, 1999) © 1999 by Mary Corpening Barber and Sara Corpening Whiteford: Chèvre Champignons, Nutty Napoleons, Seashells

From *The Complete Meat Cookbook* by Bruce Aidells and Denis Kelly (Houghton Mifflin, 1998) © 1998 by Bruce Aidells and Denis Kelly: Barba Yianni's Grilled Lamb, Grilled Pork Tenderloin with Rosemary and Fennel Seed Crust, Lime-Pickled Red Onions, Lisa's Lazy Pot Roast

From *The El Paso Chile Company Margarita Cookbook* by W. Park Kerr (William Morrow, 1999) © 1999 by W. Park Kerr: Charred Tomato Salsa Borracho, Grilled Chicken Tortas

From *The El Paso Chile Company's Sizzlin' Suppers* by W. Park Kerr (William Morrow, 1998) © 1998 by W. Park Kerr: Grilled New Potatoes in Garlicky Mustard Crust, Grilled Salmon Salad Niçoise

From *Entertaining on the Run* by Marlene Sorosky (William Morrow, 1994) © 1994 by Marlene Sorosky: Citrus Caesar Dressing, Roast Breast of Turkey with Cornbread, Spinach, and Pecans

From *Fast Appetizers* by Hugh Carpenter and Teri Sandison (Ten Speed Press, 1999) © 1999 by Hugh Carpenter and Teri Sandison: Marinated Goat Cheese with Garlic, Basil, and Orange Zest, Quesadillas with Barbecued Meat and Brie, Wok-Seared Beef in Endive Cups

From *The Great Ribs Book* by Hugh Carpenter and Teri Sandison (Ten Speed Press, 1999) © 1999 by Hugh Carpenter and Teri Sandison: Baby Back Pork Ribs with Spicy Peanut Butter Slather

From *The Hole in the Wall Gang Cookbook* by Paul Newman and A.E. Hotchner (Simon and Schuster, 1998) © 1998 by the Hole in the Wall Gang Fund, Inc.: Easy Kid Kabobs, Tic-Tac-Toe Quesadillas

From *The Italian Country Table* by Lynne Rossetto Kasper (Scribner, 1999) © 1999 by Lynne Rossetto Kasper: Chocolate Polenta Pudding Cake, Garlic-Caper Grilled Pork Chops, Potato "Gatto," Shepherd's Salad, Sicilian Sauce

From *James McNair's Favorites* by James McNair (Chronicle Books, 1999) © 1999 by James McNair: Corn-Wrapped Salmon and Scallops, Lemon Sponge Pudding Cake with Fresh Berries, Peanutty Coleslaw, Tuscan Creamy Sweet Pepper Soup

From *A Klutz Guide: Classic Cookies* by Suzanne Gooding (Klutz, 1999) ©1999 by Klutz, Inc.: Mega-Ultra-Incredicookies, Snickerdoodles

From *Marcella Cucina* by Marcella Hazan (HarperCollins Publishers, 1997) © 1997 by Marcella Hazan: Baked Tomatoes Stuffed with Salmon, Garlic, and Capers, Goat Cheese, Chive, and Chili Pepper Sauce for Pasta, Simple Veal Pasta Sauce

ACKNOWLEDGMENTS

When the idea for "Home Cooking" was just an idea on paper, the folks at KitchenAid Portable Appliances immediately saw the potential of bringing, through national television, the best culinary experts into peoples homes on a weekly basis. After all, even the best appliances need good cooking skills and great recipes to go along with them. Now, with four successful seasons on the air, KitchenAid continues to support Home Cooking and the diverse group of talented authors it features. We owe a great deal of thanks to Brian Maynard who has supported the project in countless ways with his leadership, vision, and the overriding mission of educating consumers to be better cooks. A special thank you also goes to Ken Kaminski and the many others at KitchenAid who have supported Home Cooking.

Hats off also to our exuberant and talented host, Amy Coleman, who has graciously welcomed guests into the Home Cooking studio kitchen, making them feel at home, and working with them side by side to prepare all those wonderful dishes. Her hard work, dedication, and knowledge continue to shine through at all times and make the programs fun and interesting to watch.

We are also very grateful to the numerous companies who have provided invaluable support to the project: The Weber-Stephen Products Co., Safeway Food & Drug, Beaulieu Vineyards, Glen Ellen Winery, Oxo Good Grips, Folia-Botanicals, Villeroy & Boch, Steelite, Chicago Metallic, Catskills Craftsmen, Cost Plus World Market, Emile Henry, Norpro, Pyrex, Lancaster Colony, and Sur La Table.

We'd also like to thank our hard-working staff who devotes long hours to the countless details and tasks involved in putting together a television series like this. We are grateful to each and everyone of them for their dedication and good spirit: Vené Franco, Dave Swanston, Rhonda Blewett, Rebecca Selengut, Diane Carmel, Regina Mitchell, Mike Shiota, and Daniel Dahl.

—Marjorie Poore and Alec Fatalevich

Home Cooking with Amy Coleman © 2000 by Marjorie Poore Productions
Photography by Alec Fatalevich

Design and Production: Kristen Wurz and Kari Perin
Editor: Jennifer L. Newens

ISBN 0-9651095-7-7
Printed in Hong Kong through Global Interprint

10 9 8 7 6 5 4 3 2 1

MPP Books
363 14th Avenue, San Francisco, California 94118

The **KitchenAid**® Story

A HUMBLE BEGINNING *The modern KitchenAid stand mixer began with a single drop of sweat off the end of a busy baker's nose. The year was 1908, and Herbert Johnston, an engineer and later president of the Hobart Manufacturing Company in Troy, Ohio, was watching the baker mix bread dough with an age-old iron spoon. To help ease that burden, Johnston pioneered the development of an eighty-quart mixer. By 1915 professional bakers had an easier, more thorough, and more sanitary way of mixing their wares.*

In fact, that amazing, labor-saving machine caught on so quickly that the United States Navy ordered Hobart mixers for its three new battleships—The California, The Tennessee, and The South Carolina. By 1917 the mixer was classified as "regular equipment" on all U.S. Navy ships.

The success of the commercial mixer gave Hobart engineers inspiration to create a mixer suitable for the home. But World War I interfered, and the concept of a home mixer was put on hold.

1919

THE BIRTH OF A KITCHEN ICON

1919 was truly a time of change. The gray days of war were giving way to the gaiety of the Roaring Twenties. The spark of women's suffrage had ignited and women across America would soon earn the right to vote. America was on the brink of an era of peace and prosperity, and progress was the cry from the factory to the farm.

War munitions plants across the country were busily converting to peace-time production. Meanwhile, a small manufacturing company in a sleepy, southwest Ohio town revived its effort to design the first electrical "food preparer" for the home.

And so it did! The first home stand mixer was born in 1919 at the Troy Metal Products Company, a subsidiary of the Hobart Manufacturing Company. The progeny of the large commercial food mixers, the Model H-5 was the first in a long line of quality home food preparers that utilized "planetary action." Planetary action was a revolutionary design that rotated the beater in one direction while moving it around the bowl in the opposite direction.

The wives of Troy executives tested the initial prototypes. While discussing possible names for the new machine, one homemaker commented, "I don't care what you call it, but I know it's the best kitchen aid I have ever had!" Hence, a brand name was born, and the first KitchenAid stand mixer was unveiled to the American consumer.

> ## "I don't care what you call it, but I know it's the best kitchen aid I have ever had!"

The KitchenAid H-5 rolled off the newly founded KitchenAid Manufacturing Company's assembly line at the rate of four per day and was priced at $189.50. The overriding concern then, as now, was that every KitchenAid produced would be of unsurpassed quality. Nothing would be shipped to customers that was not tested and retested.

But retail dealers were reluctant to undertake the selling of the unique "food preparer." So KitchenAid set out to sell its stand mixers door-to-door with a largely female sales force (strong enough to carry the 65-lb. Model H-5 on sales calls). Homemakers were encouraged to invite friends to their homes, where the KitchenAid salesperson would prepare food for the group showcasing the new stand mixer. By the 1930s the KitchenAid had earned wide acceptance, and dealers began to show interest.

1920–1930s
MEETING THE CONSUMERS' NEEDS

In the mid-1920s production had increased to five mixers per day, which was considered excellent efficiency by the standards of the day. Prices had declined to $150 (approximately $1,500 in today's dollars), and the company offered an easy payment program of 10% down and 10% per month for 10 months with no interest.

By the late 1920s American kitchens were growing smaller. KitchenAid responded with a smaller, lighter stand mixer at a lower price. The Model G proved so popular that the Model H-5 was stopped.

1930s

The 1930s brought the Depression, and with it, rising unemployment. The model G was beyond the financial means of most Americans, so KitchenAid confronted the problem. Within three years Kitchen-Aid introduced three new models that were less expensive and within the means of many American households.

In the midst of the great dust bowl years, social upheaval, and joblessness, KitchenAid planners laid a solid foundation that would support the stand mixer's growth for the next six decades. KitchenAid recruited Egmont Arens, a nationally acclaimed editor and world-renowned designer, to design three new stand mixer models. Arens's designs were so timelessly simple and functional that they remain virtually unchanged to this day.

1937
THE MODEL K

The Model K, first introduced in 1937, was more compact, moderately priced ($55), and capable of powering all the attachments. Every model introduced since has allowed for fully interchangeable attachments—a tribute to common sense and management of resources.

By the late 1930s, demand for KitchenAid stand mixers was so great that the factory could not keep up and sold out before Christmas each year. But in 1941 World War II intervened and the plant focused its production on munitions. During the war years there was limited production of KitchenAid stand mixers.

As peace arrived and the troops came home, production of the KitchenAid stand mixer began again in earnest. KitchenAid moved to Greenville, Ohio, to expand the production. Greenville, is still the home of the factory where the dedicated employees of that community have proudly produced the stand mixer, and now other KitchenAid products, for more than half a century.

1950—1997
SEEN IN ALL THE BEST PLACES

KitchenAid, always in the forefront of trends, introduced daring new colors at the 1955 Atlantic City Housewares Show. The new colors—Petal Pink, Sunny Yellow, Island Green, Satin Chrome, and Antique Copper—were a bold departure from the white appliances seen in most kitchens of the time. To this day KitchenAid offers the standard classics, along with a variety of decorative colors.

Today, the legacy of quality lives on not only in the multifunctional stand mixer, but also in a full line of kitchen appliances sold across the world. Every product that carries the KitchenAid name, whether purchased in Paris or Peoria, is guaranteed to be strong, reliable and versatile—each backed by over 75 years of quality and excellence.

The distinctive silhouette of KitchenAid appliances can be seen in some of America's most famous home and restaurant kitchens. "Home Cooking" with Amy Coleman—which KitchenAid is proud to sponsor as part of an ongoing commitment to nurturing the talents of home chefs—marks the latest of many cooking shows that have relied on KitchenAid appliances to perform faultlessly and enhance the decor of their sets. Viewers of "Friends," "Cybill," and other television shows will see the appliances prominently displayed, and even used on occasion, in these sitcom kitchens. And finding a top restaurant without at least one hard-working KitchenAid stand mixer would be a real challenge.

Even museums, the ultimate showcases for design excellence, feature KitchenAid products on display. San Francisco's avant-garde Museum of Modern Art, for example, featured the KitchenAid stand mixer in an exhibit of American icons. There is even a KitchenAid stand mixer in the esteemed collection of the Smithsonian Institution.

From humble beginnings among the cornfields of southwest Ohio, the name KitchenAid has become synonymous with quality. Although over the years KitchenAid has streamlined and updated its stand mixer design and technology, the worldwide success of KitchenAid can be traced to the solid foundation set back in 1919.